SOUTH WITH
ENDURANCE

Shackleton's Antarctic Expedition 1914–1917

THE PHOTOGRAPHS OF FRANK HURLEY

BLOOMSBURY

First published in Great Britain 2001
Copyright © 2001, 2004 by Book Creation Ltd., London
This edition published in 2004

The moral right of the authors has been asserted
Bloomsbury Publishing Plc, 38 Soho Square, London, W1D 3HB

A CIP catalogue record for this book is available from the British Library

Photography permissions:
Still photographs by Frank Hurley reproduced under license from the Royal Geographical Society, London,
    curator of the original glass-plate negatives since 1929. All rights reserved.
Green Album photographs copyright © Scott Polar Research Institute, University of Cambridge. All rights reserved.
Paget Colour Plates by Frank Hurley reproduced by permission of the Image Library, State Library of New South
    Wales. All rights reserved.

Individual picture credits appear on page 244.

Contributors and consultants:
Paul Costigan, Michael Gray, Shane Murphy, Gael Newton, and Joanna Wright

Special thanks are due to the following:
Joanna Wright, Curator of Photography, Royal Geographical Society Picture Library, for assisting in the selection
    of pictures and whose idea for a "Complete Collection" of Hurley's photographs made this book possible.
Shane Murphy, whose encyclopedic knowledge of Frank Hurley's work in Antarctica has been of outstanding help
    to us in the preparation of this book.
Lucy Martin, Picture Library Manager, Scott Polar Research Institute; and Ian Bolton, Anatomy Department,
    University of Cambridge for their help in scanning photographs from the *Green Album*.
Toni Mooy-Hurley, Adelie Hurley and the State Library of New South Wales, for allowing access to and
    permitting reproduction of quotations from Frank Hurley's diaries.

Published by arrangement with Book Creation Ltd., London, and Book Creation LLC, New York
Publishing Directors: Hal Robinson and John Kelly

Editor: Tamiko Rex
Designer: Peter Laws
Copy editors: Janice Anderson and Marilyn Inglis
Editorial assistant: Laura de Selincourt

Manufactured in China

ISBN 0-7475-7534-7

10 9 8 7 6 5 4 3 2 1

SOUTH WITH
ENDURANCE
Shackleton's Antarctic Expedition 1914–1917

CONTENTS

FOREWORD

FRANK HURLEY'S EXTRAORDINARY PHOTOGRAPHS taken on Sir Ernest Shackleton's Imperial Trans-Antarctic Expedition 1914–17 are now known throughout the world. His images have given readers of this dramatic story visual proof of the disaster that befell the *Endurance*. Frozen in the Antarctic ice for months, finally crushed, leaving the crew stranded on the ice floes of the Weddell Sea, the only hope of survival was a journey by small boats to Elephant Island. It is such an amazing story that, without Hurley's photographs, it would somehow be unbelievable. Yet, even when confronted with the pictures that survive this epic tale, one is still astonished that it did happen and that against all odds the crew did survive. So too, against all odds, did the photographs by Frank Hurley.

Today, this material is housed in three institutions. The Picture Library at the Royal Geographical Society in London holds the saved original glass and film negatives taken by Hurley during the expedition. The Scott Polar Research Institute in Cambridge houses the *Green Album*, a collection of prints produced while Hurley was on the *Endurance*. The State Library of New South Wales in Sydney has the Paget Colour Plates produced by Hurley.

Hurley was a professional photographer. His determination to capture the progress of the expedition on film is remarkable. Right up until the final moment before the rescue of Shackleton's men from Elephant Island, with only three exposures of film left, Hurley was alert, ready with his camera to record the event. Throughout the unfolding drama, members of the crew commented on his dedication, his absolute involvement in his work, to the extent that he would rather take photographs than play football! But it is because of his commitment to the art of photography and his knowledge of this craft that the legacy we are left with is so magnificent. It is very easy for it to appear so because of the story for, without doubt, the *Endurance* tale is breathtakingly adventurous, but it is not only the story that makes these images important. The images in this book are the product of a very fine photographer, whose photographs are not just recordings of an event that happened, but are carefully constructed works of art.

Before setting off for Antarctica, Hurley gathered his tools, from large-plate cameras to the magnesium flash flares needed to light his night photographs. He set up a darkroom on board the *Endurance* and when he was not busy taking photographs he was industrious in his darkroom, developing and printing negatives. Hurley was an artist who understood the tools of his craft and used them to create remarkable and abiding images. The conditions in which he made these images were extreme, yet repeatedly Hurley appears to have put himself in extra danger, through his passion for capturing the perfect image. He describes this in his book *Argonauts of the South*: "In my keenness to secure records of these efforts and of the ship charging the ice, I

"Hurley captured vistas from unlikely and precarious locales; the edge of a yardarm or the tip of the bowsprit while at sea, all while carrying up to 100 pounds of bulky equipment."

had a narrow escape from being crushed to death. Putting my camera in a waterproof case, I stood on a floe immediately in the vessel's path."

That Hurley was adventurous and coped very well with primitive conditions, should not overshadow his ability to create substantial and artistic photographs. He also demonstrated an exceptional ability to embrace new technology in the ever-evolving medium of photography; the State Library of New South Wales's Paget Colour Plates seen in this book are rare examples of this, an early color process that Hurley was happy to experiment with and develop. Images from his *Green Album* at the Scott Polar Research Institute give us a glimpse of a work of art in progress. In this album, Hurley busily juxtaposes images, cutting them to fit his personal story and producing prints from glass negatives that in time he would have to destroy. On looking through the images that did not survive (Hurley smashed more than 400 negatives), one feels that he must have had to make very hard choices and that smashing them to pieces was the only way that he could leave them behind. The negatives that were not destroyed now reside at the Royal Geographical Society. The fragile beauty of light and darkness that a glass negative displays is a wonder, but the fact that these negatives have traveled through such icy and tempestuous seas somehow elevates them to another plane. They are still intact, still beautiful and still capable of producing very good photographic prints nearly one hundred years later. It is a credit to Hurley and his skill that this is the case.

It is to the credit of Shackleton and his crew that they still exist, for there must have been many occasions during their struggle when lugging the weight of the glass plates and film must have appeared secondary to their survival. Even during the treacherous journey from the ice floes to Elephant Island, when the small boats were too low in the water for safety, and all non-essentials (including some precious food supplies) had to be jettisoned, they decided that Hurley's photographs and negatives should be kept. Looking at the photographs, one begins to understand their readiness to sacrifice to save these pictures. In the image on page 125, Hurley and surgeon Alexander Macklin are shown relaxing in the "Billabong" they shared with McIlroy and Hussey, with numerous photos from their journey displayed around them. Hurley's images had become part of their everyday world: They put them on their walls, and they saw themselves through his lens.

This book brings together the best examples of the images taken by Hurley during the *Endurance* Expedition. Seeing them all together is to experience the expedition through the eyes of Frank Hurley— a very professional photographer to the end.

Frank Hurley in his Burberry sledging outfit. This photo is usually regarded as a studio portrait, but it may have been taken by Thomas Orde-Lees in Antarctica on February 7, 1915, a day when Hurley photographed many of the men on board Endurance.

JOANNA WRIGHT
Former Curator of Photography
Royal Geographical Society Picture Library

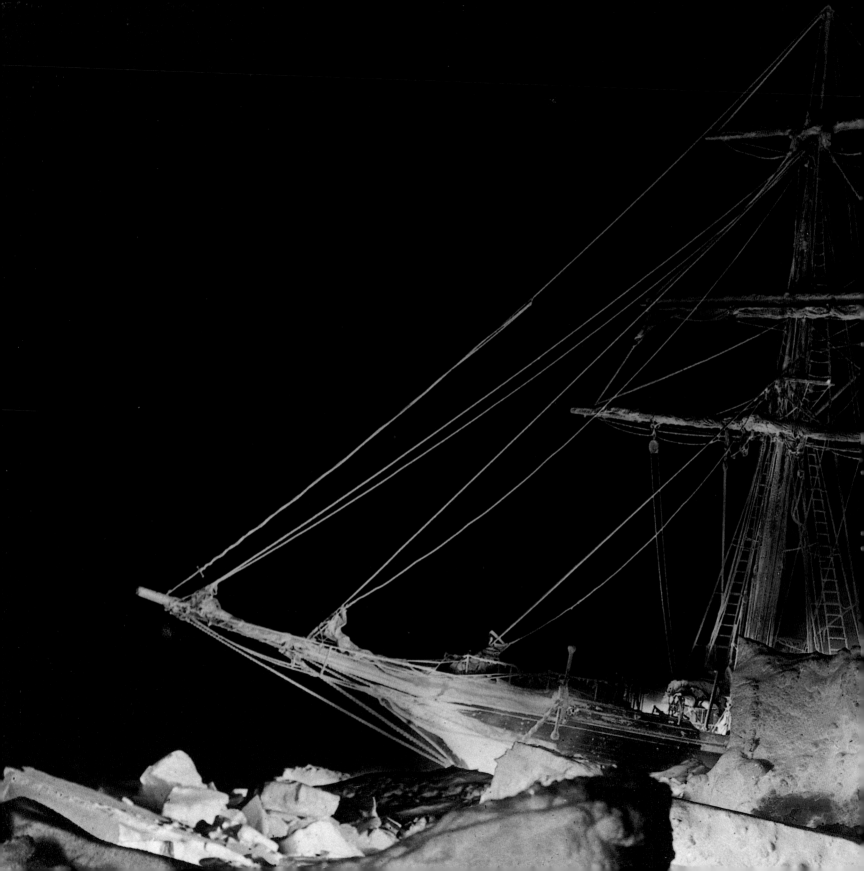

SECTION ONE
THE ENDURANCE
EXPEDITION

THE ENDURANCE EXPEDITION

SHANE MURPHY

Frank Hurley took this picture of the Endurance *stuck fast in the ice of the Weddell Sea on January 25, 1915.*

> *"3 June, 1916.*
> *My darling,*
>
> *I can only write a line as the mail is coming in and I am rushed to death with cables and arrangements for the relief of our people: I have had a year and a half of hell: and am older of course but so no lives have been lost, though we have been through what no other Polar Expedition has done…"*

SO WROTE SIR ERNEST SHACKLETON to his wife Emily from Port Stanley, Falkland Islands, after failing in a first attempt to rescue 22 of the men from his Imperial Trans-Antarctic Expedition stranded on Elephant Island, a small glacial rock near the tip of the Antarctic Peninsula.

Three and a half months later those same men remained stranded on the same bleak spit of Precambrian gravel surrounded by ice-choked seas, sheltering in a grimy little "hut" illuminated by greasy, blubber-burning lamps. They were far from shipping lanes where anyone would search for them. Believing that Shackleton, the "Boss," had died sailing to South Georgia for their relief in an absurdly small lifeboat, the castaways had surrendered all hope of rescue.

Then Shackleton appeared and saved them. That is what Shackleton did best: Materializing in body and soul when everything seemed lost.

Frank Wild, Shackleton's second in command, illustrated the man's mythological energy and leadership qualities while writing about the British Antarctic Expedition aboard *Nimrod*, 1907–09, which Shackleton outfitted and led, later being knighted for the campaign. The expedition's physical accomplishments were the first ascent of Mount Erebus and the discovery of the South Magnetic Pole and the Beardmore Glacier. Shackleton's goal, however, was to make himself the first man in history to stand at the South Pole, an attempt which only just failed. Shackleton and his party of Wild, Dr. Eric Marshall and Jameson Adams had sledged to within 100 miles (160 km) of the spot but, short of food, were forced to turn back. Late in the homeward march, long overdue at their destination, Hut Point, Marshall came down with severe diarrhea. He was left in a tent under Adams's care while Shackleton and Wild raced across the ice for help.

"Shackleton's first instructions to Captain Evans [of the *Nimrod*] were to prepare a sledge and equipment and choose three of the fittest men on board to go back with him and bring in Marshall and Adams. Shackleton asked me if I would like to go," penciled Wild, "and I said 'Yes, if you stay aboard as there is no need for two of us.' He replied, 'I must go.' In three hours the party set off, and as I stood on the bridge watching them away, Captain Evans remarked, 'Shackleton is a good goer, eh!' I replied somewhat forcibly in the affirmative; he said then 'Ah well, he has a party there that will see him out.' I said wait until they get back.

"The party Evans had chosen were [Douglas] Mawson, [Dr. A. F.] Mackay, and an athletic stoker he considered would wear them all down and remain fresh.

"Forty eight hours later all hands were astonished to see the party, including Adams and Marshall, waving for a boat from Hut Point. In a few minutes they were aboard. McKay fell into the wardroom crying out to the ship's doctor, 'Into thy hands Oh Doc, I deliver my body and my spirit!' He and Mawson went to bed for two days, the all round athletic stoker went to bed for five days, and Shackleton went on the bridge and conned the ship out of the Bay.

"Worn down to a degree almost unbelievable by a march of 1740 [miles], pulling a sledge 1,400 of those miles, on scant rations for three months, Shackleton finished up by doing 99 miles in three days."

The more lasting impression of Ernest Shackleton's willpower, perseverance, and leadership comes from the Imperial Trans-Antarctic Expedition (ITAE)—the *Endurance* saga—the greatest survival story of all time. The ITAE's schedule was boldly aggressive. Since the Pole had been conquered by Roald Amundsen, Shackleton would traverse the continent, crossing the Pole as he went! In the Antarctic spring of 1914 he planned to land at Vahsel Bucht (Bay) in the Weddell Sea and sledge an estimated 1800 miles (2880 km) across Antarctica, ending in the Ross Sea at his old *Nimrod* base. The itinerary called for six sledges pulled by dog teams driven by six ITAE members. It also required two ships, one for each sea.

Aurora, a 600-ton sealer, was purchased (with stores) from Sir Douglas Mawson for £3,200 for operations in the Ross Sea. She sailed from Hobart, Tasmania on Christmas Eve, 1914. The *Endurance* (née *Polaris*), built in Sandefjord, Norway for summer work in the Arctic, was ideal for navigating brash ice off Spitzbergen. Her hull was V-shaped, steep and thick. Fitted as a 350-ton barkentine, she was powered by a triple-expansion engine capable of 10 knots. *Polaris* cost £11,600 and was brand-spanking new when delivered to London in June of 1914. Rechristened *Endurance* after the motto emblazoned across Shackleton's family crest, "By Endurance We Conquer," she lay at berth freshly painted, about to begin her first and only voyage.

Although Shackleton was always strapped for expedition funds, he now had an even greater problem. It was clear, from events across the Channel, that war was about to erupt throughout Europe. Calling his men together in London, Shackleton stated they were free to join the war effort and then placed his ship, its stores and staff at the Admiralty's disposal. The Admiralty declined this offer, as did most of the crew.

On August 8, 1914, four days after Germany invaded Belgium and Britain declared war on Germany, *Endurance* sailed from Plymouth bound for Buenos Aires. After docking there in early October, the Australian Frank Hurley,

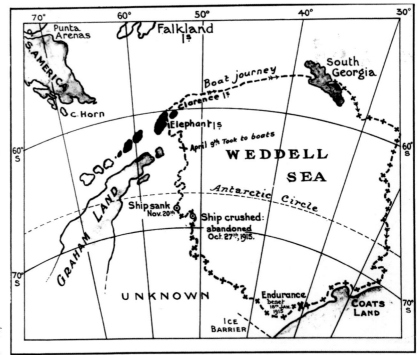

TRACK OF ENDURANCE + — + — + —   TRACK OF BOATS — — — — —

This map summarizes the Endurance *saga. It shows the ship's track before she became beset in the ice, the subsequent journey of the three boats to Elephant Island, and the* James Caird's *voyage back to South Georgia.*

who had previously been to Antarctica with Mawson (1911–14), joined ship as ITAE photographer. Hurley's enormous energy, quality of work, and reputation as a cinematographer led Shackleton to hire him sight unseen, by cable, after Hurley had applied for the position earlier in the year. Shackleton had been further motivated by selling the rights to Hurley's photographic work to help clear the expedition's debts.

To the ringing cheers of well-wishers and the strains of "God Save the King," *Endurance* slipped Buenos Aires in fine weather on October 26 with a manifest of 27 men (her manifest became 28; see below and page 31, where the Manifest is set out). After recording the scene on film, Hurley wondered on paper what the future would bring. Even if he had known, it is still likely that he would have remained aboard. There was no stopping him. Hurley lived a full 76 years, enjoying an extremely active and productive life straight up until the day he died. But, as was characteristic of him, Hurley also had a separate agenda. After the ship weighed anchor, one expedition member wrote in his diary, "Hurley practically put a pistol at Shackleton's head, saying he did not come for the salary [about £300 a year] but for a share. Shackleton could not afford to lose him so agreed."

The *Endurance*'s hold contained enough provisions for two years: An enormous amount of compressed vegetables, hut lumber, coal for the ship and hut, canned meats, and voluminous other supplies. Also tucked away below decks was 19-year-old Perce Blackborow, a stowaway who was discovered the following afternoon after the

The pastor and managers of whaling stations were entertained at lunch on board Endurance *at Grytviken on November 12, 1914.*

men had posted letters home at the Recalda Lightship and the ship was at sea beyond sight of land. Wild wrote that when he fetched Blackborow to Shackleton's cabin, the "Boss" let loose a fusillade of rough language on the boy, in the end barking, "Do you know that on these expeditions we often get very hungry, and if there is a stowaway available, he is the first to be eaten?" Blackborow, eying Shackleton's stout figure, quietly replied, "They'd get a lot more meat off you, sir." Shackleton then turned to Wild, saying, "Take him to the bo'sun. Introduce him to the cook first."

Above decks were found such innovations as three motorized sledges stored in large wooden boxes surrounded by dogs chained in kennels nailed amidships against the rails. Thomas Orde-Lees, motor expert (later storekeeper) described one sledge to a reporter: "The largest is fifteen long and four and a half feet wide. It is driven by motors and an aeroplane propeller with a 60 h.p. Anzani engine. This sledge can travel at speeds of twenty and thirty miles an hour carrying a weight of from one-half to one ton... The exhaust gases pass through a hot cupboard which is to be used for the purpose of drying sleeping bags and clothing during the day."

Captain Frank Worsley detailed the dogs in his journal. "Our 69 Huskie (from N.W. Canada) dogs are now watered 3 times & fed with one Spratts biscuit twice a day. About every half hour there is an attempt at a dog fight which has to be nipped in the bud & everytime the dogs are fed or watered pandemonium breaks out. The same happens also if a dog gets loose or is taken by the Doctors for a Lysol bath or any treatment. Two or three times a night a mornful howling dirge is started (Half their fathers are wolves)."

After crossing the Southern Ocean, the "roaring forties" (Earth's most tempestuous ocean by virtue of its coursing unimpeded around the globe's circumference), *Endurance* arrived at South Georgia on November 5, 1914. At Grytviken, a whaling settlement of 200 men and one woman, Shackleton confirmed what the Buenos Aires *Herald* had already told him: Ice conditions were severe in the Weddell Sea. The whalers, especially Thoralf Sørlle,

Endurance has her first encounter with the Weddell Sea pack-ice, December 1914.

encouraged a month's lay-over, which Shackleton endorsed, and the dogs were tethered on shore where they broke the lines and chased pigs and horses for amusement. Sørlle had grown up in Sandefjord, knew all about the *Endurance*, and predicted she would be crushed by the ice because she could not roll up and away from Antarctic pressure ridges as had Amundsen's *Fram,* with her rounded hull.

After loading additional supplies of food, coal, and winter clothing from the island's whaling stations, *Endurance* steamed from Cumberland Bay on December 5, 1914, bound for the Weddell Sea. The following day the ship was surrounded by large bergs. About 5:00 p.m. the next day she butted heads with the Weddell Sea pack-ice which became so dense as severely to retard progress. So it would be, with few exceptions, for the next several weeks, until January 19, 1915, when Shackleton and his men found themselves within sight of their goal—and, due to the gale they had just weathered in the lee of a berg, locked immovably in ice.

Hurley finally admitted the obvious on January 28, noting that a fall in temperature had caused what open water remained around the ship completely to congeal. They were, he reasoned, not going anywhere. Their last hope for a breakout came on February 14, the eve of Shackleton's 41st birthday, when an opening in the ice 300 yards (274 m) ahead gave hope.

Harry McNish, the ship's carpenter, noted events in his diary: "...started the engines & began to break up the pool [of young ice] we got through 300 ft & stoped at midnight." The next day, "Chips" McNish continued, in his idiosyncratic spelling and grammar, "Turned out 7-30 had breakfast started to break away the ice ahead but found it

Shackleton standing in a newly frozen lead.

getting to thick so we gave it up at noon for it runs from 12 to 18 ft thick so we will have to wait Gods will to get out tempreture +2."

The following day McNish marked out a soccer field on the floe. That afternoon, according to Orde-Lees, who was an odd and curious character usually dressed in a coat and necktie, everyone played soccer except "Hurley, who never plays games ... was busy with his cinematograph and cameras all the time and the pictures promise to be interesting, showing one phase of our strange existence."

On February 24 Shackleton "put everyone off watch & ship routine so that we practically cease being a ship & become a winter station," recorded Worsley. "All hands are on all day & sleep all night [except for a] Watchman who looks after the dogs & ship & keeps his eyes opened for any signs of a possible crack in the ice or an improbable fire – touch wood, from 8 p.m. to 8 a.m.... Today all hands work ... in securing & cutting up seals or clearing ships stern & after hold and stores checked, so that we may know how we stand for a siege by the Antarctic winter."

The dogs were moved off ship and their kennels were reconstructed on the ice, which was more toil than anticipated. Worsley took a crew and built "Dogloos [made from] large blocks of ice we have sawn out round the stern & thinner sheets that we cut out today of two days old young ice. The sides consist of 3 blocks each of ice & the back of hummocks picked into a vertical face. Over this we place boards or sealskins frozen harder than a board." After all the animals were comfortably housed, Wild, the doctors, James McIlroy and Alexander Macklin, Second Officer Tom Crean, artist George Marston, and Frank Hurley divided them into six equitable teams. Training in harness began immediately.

A full complement of winter clothing was issued to all hands. Rickers, extensions for the wireless receiver (a gift from the Argentine government), were spread aloft and far afield to receive Morse code signals. Despite the enormous effort spent constantly repitching the rickers in freezing temperatures, high winds and blizzards, dots and dashes were never heard.

With winter fast approaching, the hold was converted into living cubicles; they would be warmer than the cabins on the main deck. With the addition of a stove for heating and a long table for work and meals, the affair was termed "the Ritz." Lots were drawn for roommates, physicist Reginald James noting that he drew Orde-Lees, who took the top bunk where he maintained his extensive diary.

Worsley, Wild, Marston, and Crean converted the Wardroom,

The last attempt at a breakout: Poling ice away from the star- board side of the ship, February 14–15, 1915.

"At 4pm we had a
grand cinema football
match, with two full teams
of eleven a side…"
Thomas Orde-Lees
noted in his diary on
February 16, 1916.

terming their quarters "the Stables" after the small equestrian-like stalls that made up their bunk spaces. Shackleton claimed Worsley's cabin aft. Elsewhere, Hurley converted the ship's refrigerator, which sat in the lower hold behind the triple-expansion engine, into a darkroom. When not training his dog team or engaged with other assignments allotted by Wild, he would be found here developing his movie film—which required 40 gallons (182 l) of fresh water for every 10 feet (3 m) of film—then hanging the film to dry using Shackleton's paraffin heater. Here, too, Hurley maintained his diary, played chess with Reginald James, which both were learning with the aid of the *Encyclopedia Britannica*, or developing his glass plates and printing the results, at the same time constructing a photograph album of the expedition. This work survives today as the Scott Polar Research Institute's fabled *Green Album*, which was scanned to make many of the reproductions in this book. Having been mostly assembled on board, it is the only quasi-contemporaneous visual record of the expedition before the ship was crushed.

By April, as the days grew short, dark, and much colder, the dog teams had assumed a semblance of operational integrity, the crew exercised regularly around the ship, weather permitting, and one of the motor sledges was lifted overboard onto the ice and given a maiden voyage. After Hurley filmed the contraption crawling uncertainly across the ice, it broke down, McNish noting, "Lees … has no practicle experience of motors so Hurley is doing his repairs."

Frozen fast in the ice, captured by its viscous currents, on April 16 came a near collision with Crevasse Berg, an enormous chunk of ice on a crash course with *Endurance*. "Lat 75-54 Temp plus 8 we had rather a narrow squeak with a berg this morning," wrote McNish. "It passed us about half a mile away going NE it caused a lot of pressure but it is well away now."

Hurley included this photo in his Green Album, *with the caption "A meeting of the hounds out on the sea ice."*

On Saturday, May 1, 1915, misty and overcast with snow, Worsley got "the last possible glimpse" of the sun. That evening, he went on, after the customary Saturday night toast to "Sweethearts & Wives," "we make merry in the Ritz. Greenstreet gives very fine interpretation of 'Lord Effingham' with an eye glass & afterwards, with the aid of a little soot on his beard, of Charcot. Thus ornamented he is supported by a motley looking crowd of toughs foremost amongst whom is Hussey with a bogus black eye & a small boy called 'Tommy' with a squeaky voice who on other occasions if kindly spoken to answers to the name of Wild. The whole of this brigade sweeps down on Sir E's cabin serenading him with doubtful music & still more doubtful songs. After some slight disorder they are persuaded, with chocolates, to depart & annoy other peaceful members of the expedition..."

In mid-June, the coldest, darkest part of any Antarctic winter, after a fine morning spent exercising the dog teams, Hurley boasted at lunch that his team was the fastest of any and was egged-on by Shackleton. Following the meal they all went out on the ice where a track was agreed to, conditions arranged, and bets laid. The next day at noon, the course illuminated by hurricane lamps and the faint flicker of a distant aurora, the Antarctic Derby Sweepstakes was run. All hands were given the day off, many dressing especially for the event. Some of the sailors, clothed as bookies, offered wagers with Antarctic currency—chocolates and cigarettes—but no one accepted their odds (6 to 4 on Wild; "evens" on Crean; 2 to 1 against Hurley; 6 to 1 against Macklin; 8 to 1 against McIlroy; Marston scratch). Hurley, sporting his sledging pennant and a red coat with a small Australian flag wrapped around his arm, came in second to Wild. But he won during a rematch on the 25th, on a technicality, when Shackleton was pitched off Wild's sledge near the finish line, Lees noting, "Wild's dogs average 11 lbs less than Hurley's so it is indisputable that his is the better team, though Hurley won the race fairly enough on technical grounds. Some of us think it would have been very sportsmanlike of him to have offered to re-run it." Shackleton was so disappointed with himself that he paid off all bets.

Midwinter's Day, June 22, which heralded the return of the sun, deserved celebration and was observed as a special holiday with generous meals fashioned from special treats. Following a grand dinner, a "smoking concert" was held on a stage built by Hurley which he illuminated with acetylene footlights housed in coffee tins.

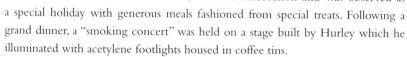

Participants pose in their costumes after the three-hour "smoking concert" on Midwinter's Day, 1915. Hussey is made up as a black minstrel, complete with banjo, and Rickenson is the "flapper" on the right. Wild, dressed as a small boy and affecting a lisp, recited "The Schooner Hesperus," aided by Hudson, costumed as the captain's daughter.

"The most outstanding feature of our concert," Lees wrote in his diary, "was undoubtedly Dr. McIlroy's daring impersonation of a semi nude demi-mondaine Spanish danseuse. Out of old velvet curtains etc. he had contrived sufficient costume to provide a somewhat decollete and abbreviated dress, but the most remarkable thing was the manner in which he had disguised his usual dark appearance and transformed himself into a blonde... As our songs are mostly topical and some satirical we did not invite the sailors in, and they of course found the usual grievance in the fact, but no doubt they also found consolation in the ample tot of rum and gifts of sweets, fruits and tobacco which Sir Ernest generously provided for them."

Late in July the sun returned, cresting the frozen landscape for nearly a minute before setting in colorful golden tints. A few days later, while entertaining themselves in another short burst of sunlight, Hurley and Macklin, noted that Worsley, "constructed some very ornate [ice] dwellings for their dogs ... Sailor's has a tapered spire rising peacefully over the entrance with an appearance like a cross surmounting it."

The next day, August 1, Sailor's "crystal palace" had been ground to powder. "Blowing a gale of Southerly wind & the floe we were in has all broken up," reads McNish's diary. "We got the dogs on board at 10-30 & every one got our warm clothes put up in as small a bundle as possible ready to get on to the floe ... we have had a start out of our monotiny if ever any one had one."

Over the next few days kennels were constructed on deck and life returned to normal, although the ship was listed five degrees to port. The crew, thinking they had seen the worst, were cautioned by Shackleton who, as Worsley recorded in his diary, told of a mouse fortified by rum who recklessly inquired, "Now, where's that damned cat?"

A new, additional dog team, made up of nearly adult pups piloted by Greenstreet, and the other teams, exercised and hunted for seals nearly every day. Dredging for specimens continued, as did meteorological and other scientific studies. Football and hockey were routinely engaged as were, McNish recorded, "Sweethearts and Wifes pressure or not" on Saturday evenings, while Sunday nights had "the Gramaphone going with all the latest songs."

But as the days lengthened and a breakout seemed imminent, the ice tightened its grip. The ship endured repeated nights of heavy pressure, the floor of the Ritz buckling while Hurley and the others, unable to sleep, lay in their bunks anticipating the ship being crushed as the wood between their cubicles cracked, groaned, and sometimes splintered. Topside, they occasionally found it difficult to perform their duties as the ship would sometimes contort like a bow, leaving ominous voids in the deck while the wood groaned and fractured around them.

At midnight on October 15, Hurley's 28th birthday, a thunderous crack compelled all hands to rush up on the slushy deck where, gazing out, they observed a widening fissure expanding through the ice. Settling into the water, the ship was suddenly free for the first time since February 15. A sail was raised and *Endurance* actually sailed—for a scant 100 yards (91 m)—before coming to rest in a narrow lead surrounded by large, menacing floes which, they knew, would eventually come together.

That happened a mere three days later when, according to Worsley, "at 4.45 p.m. the two floes which are holding us up begin to move laterally exerting pressure on the ship. Suddenly the floe on the port side cracks in huge pieces [that] shoot up from under her port bilge & in 5 or at most 7 seconds the ship heels over steadily to 30° Port List, being held under the starboard bilge by the opposing floe. The lee [life]boats are

Dawn at the close of the Antarctic winter, August 1915, after the disruption in the ice.

A stern perspective of the Endurance heeled to port.

now almost resting on the floe, the midships dog kennels break away & crash over to the lee side & the dogs howl with terror—perfect pandemonium. Everything movable flies over to the lee side of the ship & for a few moments it looks as though she will be thrown over onto her beam ends. Everybody gets to work & some order is restored, all fires are put out, battens are nailed on deck to give the dogs foothold & enable people to get about... At 8 p.m. the floes open again & in a few minutes the ship is nearly upright once more."

The end was near. On October 23, according to McNish, "we drank the health of our Sweethearts & Wifes but I am afraid we wont do so much longer as we have sprung a leak I am working all night trying to stop it the pressure is geting worse." The next day, he continued, "I have built a coffer dam in the engine room & we are still managing to keep the water down with the pumps Sir Ernest & most of the hands are packing sledges I am afraid it is all up with the ship."

On October 26, extremely heavy pressure once more assailed the ship, again opening the planking beneath the men's feet. Shackleton immediately ordered sledges, lifeboats, and emergency stores lowered onto the ice and moved away from imminent harm. With that job complete, the men returned to man the pumps throughout the night, listening to a cacophony of rupturing timbers. All hell was breaking loose. Even the penguins seemed to know it, Worsley recording a "strange occurrence ... at the instant that the heavy pressure came on the ship. [Six Emperor penguins] walked a little way towards the ship: then halted & ... proceeded to sing what sounded like a dirge for the ship."

On October 27, Worsley recorded the grand finale:

"Endurance Abandoned. First night on floe. Temp. -8.5 & 0. 22-½ h daylight. Gentle SSE to SSW breeze & clear weather. No land visible for 20 miles.

"Pressure throughout day, increasing to terrific force at 4 p.m., heaving stern up, smashing rudder, rudder post, & stern post. Decks breaking up. 7 p.m. Ship too dangerous to live in we are forced to abandon her. Water

Endurance abandoned, the men are gathered on the ice, where tents have already been erected and rescued food, clothing, and equipment lie heaped around them.

overmastering pumps & coming up to engine fires. Draw fires & let down steam. Men & dogs camp on the floe but having to shift camp twice with the floe cracking & smashing under foot get little sleep."

During this incredible series of events Shackleton called his men together. In a speech often portrayed as his most dramatic and inspiring address, one that asked the men to put aside their individual difficulties to achieve the impossible for all, he informed them of his plan to march 300 miles (480 km) across the ice to Snow Hill where he knew there was a supply of stores. He then reached into his pockets and discarded his pecuniary effects, including a gold watch and cigarette case, ordering the men to do likewise. They did, Hurley concluding that the relics of civilized refinement were entirely useless.

An extraordinary outpost of civilization: Ocean Camp in 1915.

At 3:00 p.m. on October 30 the march began after Mrs. Chippy, McNish's cat, and several young—too young—dogs were shot. The men accomplished one mile of "very hard going & we have a relay with the boats which means one for a bit & then going back for the other," noted McNish. The next day they managed three-quarters of a mile (1.2 km), using dog teams to assist with the boats; hauling was much easier that way. On the 31st they only managed to move forward a paltry half mile (0.8 km).

On the morning of November 1, after a heavy snow, they quit. Shackleton, Wild, Worsley, and Hurley ventured forth on an exploratory trip, searching out a track, but discovered the ice to be broken, unworkable, and impassable. By unanimous agreement they decided on a retreat to a solid old floe and await a breakup in the dense ice surrounding them, stretching as far as the eye could see in all directions.

During the next few days, on Hurley's suggestion, a huge chisel was designed and put in service; Shackleton himself fashioned the large blade from salvaged steel. Hung from the boom, and operated like a pile-driver, after repeated efforts it cut into the ship's partially submerged deck, allowing crates of walnuts, frozen onions, sledging rations and other foodstuffs to bob to the surface where they were retrieved by boathooks and placed on "shore." Shortly later, a second cut was made in the deck with similar results. By diligent work aided by fine weather, 4 tons of stores were in camp by November 5. On the 7th, adrift on the ice at a place they called "Ocean Camp," all were comfortably housed, McNish writing, during a blizzard, that "[Hurley and Kerr] have been rigging up a range [made by Hurley] for cooking out of the ash shoot it has turned out very well we had a fine [stew] tonight of corned meat preserved potatoes it was a treat..."

The stove made by Hurley and Kerr at Ocean Camp. Orde-Lees called it "a wonderful piece of ingenuity."

Hurley salvaged the bulk of his photographic equipment, glass plates and cinematograph film on November 2. Determined to retrieve them, he visited the wreck with Walter How and somehow cut into the refrigerator where he managed to fish out his zinc-lined galvanized tins, discovering them mostly unharmed, and returned triumphantly to camp with them.

A week later Hurley selected the pick of his negatives, about 150 he reckoned in his original diary, and, because of weight restrictions imposed by Shackleton, destroyed what he estimated to be about 400 glass negatives. His plan seems to have been to make inter-negatives of his *Green Album* photos when returning to civilization. Nearly two dozen "keepers" were Paget Colour Plates. The Paget process was a lumbering turn-of-the-century method by which color images could be captured and printed. It is interesting to note that Hurley's *Endurance* Paget Colour Plates are some of the only survivors of the medium.

On November 21, at 5:00 p.m., as the men were resting in their sleeping bags, Shackleton noticed a movement in the wreck. Calling out, he alerted the men who ran quickly from their tents to the highest vantage points available. In five minutes the stern of the *Endurance* rose vertically in the air and then dove forever beneath the ice. Most of the men were relieved at the sight: They had rescued everything of value and the wreck was, by now, quite unsafe for more salvage work.

The next day, Hurley packed his *Green Album* in a brass case and soldered on the lid, discovering, in the process, that blubber made excellent flux. He also removed the lenses from his large-plate cameras and soldered them in a tin. His days as a man with every description of camera were over. Henceforth, he would rely on his small folding Vest Pocket Kodak, and other members' cameras, for negatives.

Throughout, the men were busy preparing for the inevitable, a voyage in the three lifeboats McNish was refitting from salvaged lumber. Hurley, in addition to constructing a stove that would eventually be used on

Masts and oars set up in the snow as posts for drying lines, with clothes and blankets slung over them.

Elephant Island, fashioned a bilge pump for the largest boat, soon to be named the *James Caird*, while Lionel Rickenson made her a rudder and others cut and sewed canvas for sails. When completed, each boat was placed on a sledge, also modified by McNish. Shackleton named them *Dudley Docker*, *Stancomb-Wills*, and *James Caird,* after the expedition's primary benefactors.

A year after leaving South Georgia, now castaway on the ice under severe circumstances, they were ready, they imagined, for the open ocean. But the ice offered no escape. As December dragged on, boredom set in. Hoping to gain a strategic advantage and lift the men's spirits, Shackleton announced a second march, planning to move by night when the surface was firmest.

December 22, warm and overcast, was Midsummer's Day. Because the march would begin the following day, it was also observed as Christmas. Every last miscellaneous food item was available for the enjoyment of everyone all day long, the consequence being that, by evening, most hands had a squeaky gut. Waking on December 23, Shackleton found the weather, ice and wind set firmly against him. So was Harry McNish who, on December 27, the fifth day of toilsome marching, hauling, and sodden relaying, became insubordinate by refusing duty in his harness. Shackleton took McNish in hand and told him what his duty was. But the carpenter had made his point. After traveling eight wearying miles (12.8 km), the wind had pushed them back almost to their starting point.

The next day they retreated half a mile (0.8 km) to a flat old floe, which immediately raised a crack, necessitating the camp's removal some 100 yards (91 m) south. Camp was removed again the following day in a further retreat of three-quarters of a mile (1.2 km). This, then, was "Mark Time Camp," later to become "Patience Camp," established at the dawn of 1916. And here they sat, cold, bored, increasingly agitated, and hungry for three months waiting for the ice to open.

On January 14, after camp was shifted to another floe, "we had one of the saddest events since we left Home happen," lamented McNish. "There was 27 of our faithfull dogs shot to save our food supplies Hurley & Macklin have gone on a sledge journey to Ocean Camp to bring what food stuffs we left there." On the 16th, after muscling 900 pounds (408 kg) of supplies across six miles (9.6 km) of tortuously broken ice, Hurley rested from the journey as Wild shot his dogs behind a not-too-distant hummock. While grieving for the loss of his team, especially its leader, Shakespeare, a trusted and faithful companion, Hurley knew, as did the other expedition members, that the dogs had to die so that the men could live.

In early February, Worsley and Hurley suggested that the *Stancomb-Wills*, which had been left behind at Ocean Camp, be brought on to Patience Camp. The task was accomplished by 16 men and the remaining two dog teams. But supplies were low. Securing enough game to fill their stomachs was increasingly a problem. "We got a Weddel seal this morning which will keep the pot boiling for a few days more," scrawled McNish in his small diary. "We are still having 1 hot drink dayly as yet but we hope to get more seals soon. I smoked myself sick through trying to stifle the hunger."

On February 29, Leap Year Day, two Weddell seals were killed. Then, to celebrate Shackleton's 42nd birthday, which had gone uncelebrated on the 15th, and in recognition of their enforced celibacy, the men enjoyed a day-long bachelor's repast. Again, Shackleton pulled out all the stops, ordering seal steaks and what remained of the dried onions for breakfast, seal liver and dog biscuits for lunch, and a thick stew of jugged hare and other rare items, thrown together with the perennial "seal kidney," for a grand dinner washed down with the last of their cocoa.

Better still, as the expedition diaries indicate, open water was tantalizingly close. Now in anticipation of getting in the boats any day, the men had to endure a frustrating game of wait and see as March 1916 ground onward. But however long they waited the same thing happened: The ice would open, then close. The next day would prove uneventful in the extreme, as would many following days. To while away the hours, Shackleton and Hurley spent most afternoons playing Poker Patience using imaginary theater tickets as currency.

The galley at Patience Camp, with a screen made from canvas set on oars. McNish noted that the floor had to be built up with fresh snow every morning as the heat of the fire—a point drum with a few holes round it—melted the snow.

It was on March 30, wrote McNish, when their floe cracked in half, "we got the boats & sledges shifted & was going to have breakfast. When [the ice] cracked again under the *James Caird*. But we got her over before she fell in the ditch. & while at breakfast a sea leopard came up & went to sleep peasfully. but it was his last sleep as Wild went out & shot him. Then he shot the last of our faithful dogs. Of which we kept the five young ones for food. & Their flesh tastes a treat ... after being so long on seal meat. & this last 14 days on almost nothing. We got 20 fish in the leopard stomach & we are having them for breakfast tomorrow."

Finally, on Sunday, April 9, 1916, after 156 days on the ice, their small floe split again and they took to the boats. The allotments to the boats were: *James Caird*—Shackleton, Wild, Clark, Hurley, Hussey, James, Wordie, McNish, Green, Vincent, McCarthy; *Dudley Docker*—Worsley, Greenstreet, Kerr, Orde-Lees, Macklin, Cheetham, Marston, McLeod, Holness; *Stancomb-Wills*—Hudson, Crean, Rickenson, McIlroy, How, Bakewell, Stephenson, Blackborow. That morning, uncertainty prevailed: The ice opened and closed time and again. Then, at about 1:00 p.m., after a

The James Caird *being hauled up Providence Beach, April 15, 1916. Greenstreet and Blackborow, unable to help because of sickness, are seated in the background.*

lunch of seal hoosh (the Antarctic explorer's stew), Shackleton gave the order to launch the boats. It took a full hour—they stowed 200 boxes, including Hurley's precious plates, album, and film. The *James Caird*, under Shackleton, went first. After rowing north through heavy bergs for three miles (4.8 km) the boats passed under the lee of the pack-ice—where a vicious tidal bore surprised, chased, and nearly overtook them; only by exhaustive hard rowing did they manage to escape. At dusk, after seven miles (11.2 km) of progress, they camped on a floe which rose and fell in the heaving ocean.

The dream had come true! But they did not sleep easy. At midnight their rocking berg cracked in half, separating Shackleton's tent and the *Caird* from the rest of the camp. It also split the sailors' tent. How and Holness fell into the ocean but were quickly rescued by Shackleton. Holness, happy to be alive, had only one complaint: he'd lost his tobacco! The party was reassembled, the roll called; all members were accounted for. A blubber fire was kindled, the tents taken down. The remainder of the long, cold night was spent anticipating the morning.

At 8:00 a.m. they again took to the boats. That day, the wind got up until, about dusk, it was blowing a gale with a northeast blizzard which cut like sharp knives through the men's remnant clothing. Freezing, deprived of sleep for 48 hours, they eventually pulled up on an old 20 yards (18 m)-wide floe where they ate, camped, and retired apprehensively to their bags.

The following morning, April 11, they awoke to a terrifying spectacle—huge half-mile (0.8 km)-long ocean swells choked with icebergs repeatedly assailing what had become their ice prison. At 1:00 p.m., when their floe had considerably diminished in size and all were preparing to say good-bye to each other, an open pool of water came their way. The boats were launched and the stores quickly thrown in. That would be their last night on a floe. After the events of the previous two nights, Shackleton was determined that the three boats would remain at sea, no matter what the conditions.

During the next five horrid days, hungry, delirious with thirst, frozen to the core, and unable to sleep, they battled high waves, freezing temperatures, pack-ice, diarrhea, and seasickness in ice-encased boats and clothing. Due to vagaries in the wind and tidal currents, they were, for lack of a better word, lost, which caused reversals in direction, consequent problems in morale, and grave fears of being upset by Killer whales, great pods of which blew nearby when the boats were strung together at night. But finally, by great providence and almost by serendipity, they sighted Elephant Island 30 miles (48 km) off at dawn on April 14. They toiled at the oars for hours, approaching to within 10 miles (16 km) of the blessed landfall by 3:00 p.m. "I see a rock!" cried one. But here, nearly landed, they were gripped by an offshore current that forced the boats to remain at sea one remaining night—in a blizzard during which the *Docker* disappeared from sight and was thought lost. The *Caird* and *Wills* landed on Elephant Island on April 15 just in time. Several of the men were near death. Then the *Docker* hove in sight. All were saved!

Because their generously flat landing site was vulnerable to tidal variations, the next day Wild was sent off in a boat in search of a secure camp. McNish, with remarkable punctuation, thumb-nailed the situation: "[Blackborow's] toes are gone. Rest are getting along very well. Only Hudson who has gone of his head & both his hands are pretty bad yet. Wild & his party arrived back at 8-30. So we all turned out & hauled the boat up. He reports a fine place 7 miles from here so we are going to shift to it tomorrow."

The following day, McNish continued, was "Monday 17th We turned out early & got the boats launched at high water … right in the heart of a heavy SW squall … after that it was nothing but a succession of heavy snow squalls. Which gave us as much as we could do to keep up against them. & prevent ourselves from being blown out to sea…"

The next day, at the new camp named "Cape Wild," McNish noted, was "Wilds Birthday a Blizard on at present… No. 5 tent has blown to ribbons. & all the others are down flat on top of our sleeping bags & held there by large stones."

"Thurs April 20th," he went on, was "a better day with ocasional snow squalls. I dont think there are ever many fine days on this forlorn island. Started to dismantle the Docker to deck in the Caird which is going to South Georgia for relief as I dont think there will be many surviors if they have to put in a winter here."

Shackleton had decided on the only course of action. He would sail the *James Caird*, a whaleboat not much bigger than a Grand Banks dory (23 feet/7 m), to South Georgia, across the coldest, most violent storm-tortured ocean on earth. Calling his men together he asked for volunteers, choosing Worsley, McNish, John Vincent, Tim McCarthy, and Tom Crean—who begged to go. Many, including Shackleton, doubted they would survive the journey. He wrote to Hurley, assigning the rights to the photographs and films for 18 months and afterward full possession, should he not live. Shackleton also composed a note to Frank Wild, leaving him in charge of the Elephant Island castaways, going on to request that Wild, Hurley, and Orde-Lees write the expedition account.

Elephant Island, April 15, 1916. Land— and all were alive! This was the first touch of solid earth after a terrible and remarkable seven-day ocean voyage in the smallest boats imaginable.

At 11:00 a.m. on Easter Monday, April 24, 1916, after Worsley observed an opening in the ice and McNish had finished decking over the *Caird* with pieces of Venesta wood and canvas, she was launched. After pitching McNish and Vincent into the ocean and floating away from some onshore rocks which nearly destroyed her, the *Caird* was secured on a long painter and tendered by the *Wills*. Among the supplies loaded were McNish's adze, a Primus cooker, Shackleton's shotgun, 36 gallons (164 l) of water, 112 pounds (50.8 kg) of ice, and about a ton of rocks for use as ballast. Some of Hurley's photographs also went aboard, probably in the box made up that morning by Orde-Lees which contained Worsley's logbooks. Comprising a tantalizing part of *Endurance* minutiae, one of these photographs appeared in the London newspaper, the *Daily Mirror*, on July 10, 1916.

When the *Caird* was ready, Shackleton came ashore, had a cigarette with Wild, wished the men good-bye, and was rowed out to the *Caird* for the last time. With sails raised, she turned north and was quickly lost to view in the ocean's high swells. "Sailed at 12.30 P.," Worsley noted that evening where he sat in the *Caird*'s cramped, lilliputian hold. "Heartily cheered by shore party which we returned to full extent of our lungs. Fresh W.N.W breeze…"

Worsley's notes made during the *Caird*'s incredible journey are telling in their brevity—on terra firma he normally produced a full page every day. But aboard the *Caird*, beyond stellar observations and computations, he recorded very little. May 1, 1916, a date which saw the *Caird* nearly halfway through its historic voyage, was an exception: "D[ead]R[eckoning] 0° E[ast] 30m[iles]. 57°11'S 48°1'W Drift. SSW moderate gale; heavy lumpy sea; boat lying to sea anchor; heavily iced up. Overcast."

Incarcerated for 17 hellish days, bitterly cold, wet to the core, their boat pitching, rolling, and jerking heavily with massive waves breaking over her at all hours, often hove to and iced over, Shackleton and his crew must have felt that every minute was a full lifetime. Every day was the same—a horrid, frigid nightmare.

Worsley's notes made during the journey fail to mention the "great wave" which nearly put an end to them all. But after accomplishing the impossible—sailing 800 miles (1280 km) across the Southern Ocean in a

The James Caird is launched on Easter Monday, April 24, 1916.

tiny boat and landing on Wednesday, May 10, 1916, on the "wrong" side of South Georgia without potable water, after weathering a brutal hurricane during which a large steamer foundered with all hands somewhere nearby—Worsley brought his diary up to date: "One night I had just been relieved at the helm by Sir E & was crawling into my [frozen stiff] sleeping bag, when I heard him call out cheerily 'It's clearing to the SW' & immediately after: 'My God, it's a sea, hang on' It was a sea! We felt her hurled broadside bodily, rolling on to our beam ends & submerged in a smother of foam & water… Fortunately it was a single lonely sea that like a 'rogue' elephant had tried to catch us unawares & destroy us. When its white bulk first appeared, Sir E said it covered a fourth of the horizon & looked like a band of clear white sky to the SW. Quick hard bailing by all of us alone saved her… It was nearly 3 hours before we had her clear of water."

That notation was made at "Pegotty Camp" at the head of King Haakon Bay, where the *Caird* had been over-turned and insulated with Tussock grass. Now fed on fresh albatross and their eggs, and watered by a creek at their feet, most were regaining strength. Vincent, however, was done-in—and the *Caird* was no longer seaworthy. Shackleton's only recourse was to cross South Georgia's interior mountains, glaciers, and formidable icy crevasses, 26 miles (41 km) of unmapped ice and rock, by foot. In McNish's diary he wrote:

> "Sir,
> "I am about to try and reach Husvik on the East Coast of this island for relief for our party. I am leaving you in charge of this party consist … of Vincent, MacCarthy, yourself. You will remain here until relief arrives. You have ample seal food which you can supplement with birds & fish according to your skill. You are left with a double barrelled gun. 50 Cartridges.
> 40 to 50 Bovril sledging rations,
> 25 to 30 biscuits:
> 40 Streimers Nutfood.
>
> "You also have all the necessary equipment to support life for an indefinate period. In the event of my non return you had better after winter is over try and sail round to the East Coast.
>
> "The course I am making toward Husvik is <u>East</u> magnetic
> "I trust to have you relieved in a few days
> "Yours Faithfully
> "EH Shackleton
> "H McNish"

At 4:00 a.m. on May 19, 1916, under a calm, clear moonlight sky—rare weather on South Georgia—Shackleton, Worsley, and Tom Crean left the known world behind. After a day of misdirection and exhaustive climbing through thick, soft snow, they sat on a high ridge where a heavy sea fog enveloped them. Night was fast approaching. Shackleton decided to make a "sled" from the rope that held them together—it was that or freeze to death right where they were. Untying and curling the rope beneath themselves, away they sped into the black void below; Worsley later wrote he was never more scared in his life. After plummeting several hundred feet they tumbled into a snowbank, brushed themselves off and kept marching. They forced on through desperation ordained by sheer willpower to conquer the ongoing netherworld of jagged peaks and steep faces of slick blue ice confronting them at every turn.

Thirty-six grueling hours after leaving "Pegotty Camp" three horribly ragged men emerged from the heart of Antarctica at the door of a shocked Thoralf Sørlle. Having crossed profoundly rugged terrain using 50 feet (15.2 m) of rope and a carpenter's adze as climbing tools, with screws in their boots for crampons, they arrived to a world gone mad. Millions were dying in Europe. Only Worsley's journals remained with them. Their few sledging rations were gone; that morning, after hearing Stromness station's call-to-work whistle—the first sound of civilization in 18 months—the Primus cooker had been thrown away. Only later was the rope surrendered, after rappelling a waterfall whence they emerged soaked and nearly frozen. Then, near their goal, Crean nearly impaled himself on the adze. It was the last item to go. As part of a recent documentary on the *Endurance* expedition, three world-class mountaineers, well-fed and completely equipped, retraced the journey from "Pegotty Camp" to Stromness. It took them three days.

Already half of Stromness had fled at the horror of seeing them. Sørlle, believing the strangers to be drunken whalers, growled, "Who the hell are you?" The man in the middle stepped forward. "My name is Shackleton," he replied. Sørlle, it is said, wept at the announcement. Dressed in tattered blubber-stained clothes, terribly scarred by frostbite and utterly haggard, Shackleton, Worsley, and Crean took coffee in Sørlle's sitting room, where, among so many other things, Shackleton learned the *Aurora* had slipped her moorings, leaving his Ross Sea party in dire straits. He would have to undertake to rescue them as well.

But Elephant Island came first. However exhausted he was, that same night a freshly bathed, well-fed and warmly clothed Ernest Shackleton searched out a rescue ship while Worsley sailed off in the whaler *Samson* to retrieve McNish, McCarthy, and Vincent. The morning after the "Pegotty Camp" crew and the *James Caird* were brought in, Søren Berntsen, manager at Husvik, wrote to his wife, "It is unbelievable that anyone could survive in a small boat from South Shetland to here at this time of year. Shackleton and two of the others slept here [May 22, 1916] and I heard the two make an awful noise in their sleep—they thought they were back at sea in the small boat."

Pages from the detailed diary kept by Frank Hurley throughout the Endurance *expedition.*

On May 23, wrote Worsley, "Sir Ernest, having made arrangements for Macarthy, McNish & Vincent's return to England on the next steamer, he, Crean, & myself started from Husvik in the whaler *Southern Sky* under Captain Thom. Our decks are nearly awash as we carry enough coal to take us to Elephant I. &, once rescuing our men, to the Falklands wireless station." But the ice beat them back. Returning to Port Stanley, another attempt was made in the *Institutio de Pesca 1*. In mid-June, 18 miles (29 km) off Elephant Island, the ice again granted no approach. Then fog came down. Once more they retreated to Port Stanley, the ship's engines knocking badly.

After crossing to Punta Arenas in southern Chile, Shackleton received subscriptions of £1,500 to charter and fit-out an old oak schooner, *Emma*, which commenced her journey on July 12, towed part way by a small rusty steamer named *Yelcho*. The weather was foul; *Yelcho* soon returned to port. *Emma*'s engines broke down continually. The wind came dead ahead. The ice was worse than ever. The *Emma* had to turn back. A report in the Buenos Aires *Herald*, September 1, 1916, said that, on returning to port, Shackleton "had to be helped ashore, suffering from rheumatics, cramps, exposure, the damp, worry & cold. He seemed completely done up." Almost immediately, the Chilean government volunteered *Yelcho*, the only available boat.

By then all hope of rescue had been surrendered on Elephant Island. Their first days without Shackleton had been the most appalling. To combat the howling winds, flying bits of ice and freezing temperatures, they had begun chipping out a cave in a nearby glacier. It was soon proclaimed of little use due to the moisture that rained down on all who entered. On April 28, a hut was fashioned by overturning the *Wills* and *Docker* atop two 4 foot-(1.2 m)-high stone walls 18 feet (5.5 m) apart. Drained of energy and quickly chinking the walls with canvas, the inhabitants found themselves covered with snow the following morning. Hurley, James, and Hudson, still ensconced

in Shackleton's tent, fared better, but not for long. On the 30th, during a break in the weather, work continued on the hut. That evening, everyone called it home.

So it would be for the next five months. The passing days, most of which were remarkably similar, with snow, wind, and freezing temperatures, accumulated into weeks reckoned by the *Caird*'s departure. On most days the men would rise at 9:00 a.m., eat fried penguin steaks, retire to their bags to await a lunch of stewed penguin, retire to their bags until dinner (almost always stewed seal) and again retire to their bags—where they had been all day; then, between 5:00 and 6:00 p.m., Marston would read recipes from his small penny cookbook or they listened as Hussey tortured the banjo with what McNish had called his "six known tunes."

Save dwindling victuals, there was little variation in routine or weather. There were, however, exceptions. On days when the weather gave pause, Hurley and the others promenaded on the spit, built snow statues of well-endowed females, or played cricket using stones for balls and driftwood as wickets. During one such outing in

early June, as their second Antarctic winter descended cold and forbidding, Holness managed to catch a mackerel in his hands. He tore it apart on the spot and ate it raw.

Perhaps the most notable day during the enforced captivity at Cape Wild was June 15, when all of Blackborow's left toes were amputated, dropping from a bed of crates where he lay etherized into the bucket beneath. Despite the rain, everyone except the

"The most motley and unkept assemblage that ever was projected on plate," noted Hurley of this photo, taken on May 10, 1916 on Elephant Island.

two doctors, Wild, Hurley, and How, were sent out of the hut for three hours to entertain themselves, which they did by trading haircuts in a cave. That evening, after Blackborow had awakened, they had a loud sing-song to celebrate the successful surgery.

June 22, Midwinter's Day, warm and mild, was acknowledged with an abundant feed of extra rations at all three meals, lunch contrived from a boil of moldy nut food and sledging rations while dinner presented a hot stew of selected chopped meats, half a pound (227 g) of sugar and four sledging rations. A "smoking concert" followed, with some 30 broadsides and recitations, many accompanied by Hussey's banjo, being offered from the sleeping bags. After lights out, Orde-Lees, full as a tick, snored so loudly that he had to be kicked in the head.

But as the weary days of waiting accumulated and spring gained a foothold, the men became despondent. Many were the speculations as to the name of the rescue vessel and its arrival date—assuming Shackleton had made it to South Georgia. The few remaining optimists, ignoring the dire predictions of the others, settled on August 16 as their rescue date. The ship, it was believed, would be the *Aurora*. The *Aurora*, however, had problems of her own. Monday, August 16, passed overcast and damp with a temperature of 27°F (-2.8°C). After that, no one, from Wild on down, honestly believed that Shackleton was still alive.

By the end of August, only two cases of rations remained at the hut; starvation was at hand. Expedition Cook Charles Green later told Shackleton biographer James Fisher, "Earlier in the expedition, if anybody killed a seal, they had the brains for perks. But later, on Elephant Island, we were starving—it was suggested that we were going to have to cast lots to see which one was going to be done in first. I said to them, 'Whoever is going to be killed, I'm going to have the job of cooking him—and I want the brains...'"

Frank Wild's only remaining option was for him to orchestrate the rescue of the men under his command on Elephant Island. On August 29, Orde-Lees recorded, "Wild ... and four other members are to go in the Dudley Docker, and will make their way carefully along under the lee of the land from island to island of the South Shetlands keeping always in Bransfield Straits along their southern coasts until they reach Deception Island [where they will doubtless find whalers]."

At lunchtime the following day, Hurley and Marston were outside on the beach shelling limpets which they had speared with sticks; limpets, a recent dietary innovation on Elephant Island, were especially tasty when served with seaweed boiled into a jelly. Gazing out across the nearly ice-free ocean, a rare phenomenon indeed, Marston saw a ... ship? Marston was mistaken, Hurley replied. What he saw, said Hurley, was an iceberg. Both men looked again. They immediately cried out "Ship-O!" but no one in the hut understood their muffled screams. Then Marston came charging up the path to the "sty" yelling the news again and again and again.

Hurley gathered up some paraffin and a handful of sennegrass (a grass from Scandinavia used to insulate boots). When he struck the match the resulting explosion thundered across the water like a cannon's roar. The *Yelcho* signaled her response, and a boat was lowered. Shackleton landed, throwing cigarettes and tobacco at their feet. Like giddy school children they cheered his arrival. Wild invited him to see the hut but Shackleton was impatient to be off. In less than an hour, they were gone. That night, aboard *Yelcho*, flung side to side like a cork on the wide ocean's waves, all were raving seasick—and hysterically happy.

Arriving at Punta Arenas at 11:30 a.m. on September 3, 1916, Hurley and the others were flabbergasted—the piers were jammed with 8000 well-wishers! The band played as they came ashore and marched through the town in their filthy, blubber-stained rags. Men and women wept openly in the streets. The crowd surged around them; they were all introduced to the governor. On and on the celebrations continued, day after day. So it would be for the next several weeks, wherever they went. Shackleton's glorious failure was front page news.

Hurley, a workaholic, groused at the many social engagements suddenly thrust upon him. He preferred the confines of a local photographer's darkroom, where, he discovered on the evening of September 4, nearly all of his negatives and film had survived the ordeal and would print. (Five months later, in London, Hurley was outfitting a return trip to South Georgia to round-out his expedition photographs and film with scenes of animal life. He arrived at Leith Harbour on March 25, 1917 and departed a month later after securing 100 Paget Colour Plates, numerous monochrome prints, and 4000 feet (1219 m) of film, quite pleased with the results.)

"All saved and all well! This is one of the epics of the world," read the Buenos Aires *Herald*

The *Yelcho arrives at Elephant Island, August 30, 1916.*

with exacting prescience on September 5, 1916. "Had Shackleton lived in the days of the Vikings, the bards would have composed a saga to his praise, & would sing it in the North land by the side of roaring fires in the great halls of the mighty. They would sing how in three successive attempts the hero had to turn back flouted by wind & Ice. Perhaps the world nowadays is too utilitarian to immortalize the adventures of Shackleton & his companions in this manner. It is too busy trying to get rich, & does not count as valuable anything that does not contribute thereto. Perhaps this deed of heroism was as bold as any sung by Homer & the Norse skàld or by the troubadour: & the world must ultimately appreciate its true worth."

Unfortunately, Shackleton could not enjoy the many accolades now bestowed upon him. While he had courtesies to pay to various heads-of-state across South America, the victims of the Ross Sea disaster called him. After being fêted at numerous grand receptions, he and Worsley finally left Buenos Aires by train on October 8, 1916, bound for New Orleans by steamer, San Francisco by train, eventually arriving in Wellington, New Zealand aboard the S.S. *Moana* to commence rescue operations in the Ross Sea.

Because Shackleton's original plan was to begin his transcontinental trek directly on reaching Vahsel Bucht, *Aurora* had landed near Cape Evans, *Nimrod*'s old haunts, where the Ross Sea party successfully laid and marked depots up to 80°S during early 1915. Shackleton's further orders were, that, should he not turn up in the fall of 1915, additional depots would be placed near the Beardmore Glacier the following spring. Because of this, *Aurora* was only partially unloaded when she was ripped from her moorings by shrill winds on May 7, 1915 when she abruptly floated away in the night. After prolonged capture and much danger in the ice, the ship hobbled into Port Chalmers under a jury rudder.

Meanwhile, the 10 men stranded ashore with few supplies, inadequate clothing, and insufficient shelter, but unerringly focused on Shackleton's cause, endured the winter and heroically carried out their spring work by augmenting depot supplies with odds-and-ends unearthed at Shackleton's and Captain Scott's old huts. But among other events in the Ross Sea, Mackintosh and two others lost their lives, the survivors going cold and hungry in conditions similar to those suffered on Elephant Island. The seven remaining men were, of course, rescued by Shackleton in the refitted *Aurora* under the command of John King Davis on January 10, 1917. This date is the real end of the *Endurance* story.

Paget Colour Plates

A British-made Paget Colour outfit consisted of a pack of panchromatic black and white film, a pack of mechanical color screens, each screen being unique to each image and not interchangeable, and a pack of filter screens.

The 32 Paget Colour Plates that survived the expedition are a testament to the photographic advances of the time. C. F. Findlay's Paget Screen Colour Process was based on Lumière's Autochrome mosaic screen plate. To produce the screen elements, three equal quantities of potato starch grains were dyed respectively red, green, and blue-violet. The dyed grains were then mixed together and the whole dusted on to a glass plate covered with a sticky coating. The surplus grains were brushed off and those adhering to the plate were flattened out under pressure with any slight gaps or spaces between the individual grains filled with carbon powder. This mosaic base was coated with a thin panchromatic emulsion and the resulting plate exposed with the mosaic nearest to the lens of the camera. A detailed account of how the process worked is given in Brian Coe's book *Cameras: From Daguerreotypes to Instant Pictures*.

Ship's Manifest
Weddell Sea Party

Name	Nickname	Birthplace	Rank/Role	Name	Nickname	Birthplace	Rank/Role
Sir E. Shackleton	Boss	Ireland	Leader	Reginald James	Jimmy	England	Physicist
Frank Wild	Frankie	England	2nd in Command	George Marston	Putty	England	Artist
Frank Worsley	Skipper	New Zealand	Ship's Captain	Thomas Orde-Lees	The Colonel	England	Motor Expert
Hubert Hudson	Buddha	England	Navigating Officer	Frank Hurley	The Prince	Australia	Photographer
Lionel Greenstreet	Horace	England	First Officer	Harry McNish	Chips	Scotland	Carpenter
Tom Crean	Tom	Ireland	Second Officer	Charles Green	Doughballs	England	Cook
Alfred Cheetham	Alf	England	Third Officer	Perce Blackborow	Blackie	Wales	Steward
Louis Rickenson	Rickey	England	Chief Engineer	John Vincent	Bo'sun	England	Able Seaman
Alexander Kerr	Krasky	Scotland	Second Engineer	Timothy McCarthy	Tim	Ireland	Able Seaman
James McIlroy	Mickey	England	Surgeon	Walter How	Hownow	England	Able Seaman
Alexander Macklin	Mack	England	Surgeon	William Bakewell	Bakie	Canada	Able Seaman
Robert Clark	Bob	Scotland	Biologist	Thomas McLeod	Stornoway	Scotland	Fireman
Leonard Hussey	Uzbird	England	Meteorologist	William Stephenson	Steve	England	Fireman
James Wordie	Jock	Scotland	Geologist	Ernest Holness	Holie	England	Fireman

SECTION TWO
THE PERFECT PICTURE
JAMES FRANCIS HURLEY

THE PERFECT PICTURE:
JAMES FRANCIS HURLEY

GAEL NEWTON

JAMES FRANCIS (FRANK) HURLEY, the third of five children, was born into a working-class family from Sydney, New South Wales, on October 15, 1885 in the inner-city suburb of Glebe. By the 1880s Glebe was densely built up with a mix of workers' cottages, multi-storied terraced houses, and Italianate mansions for more affluent middle-class families. The Hurleys lived in small cottages at several locations.

Although many Hurley names appear in connection with mining in western New South Wales in the state's early days, Frank's father, Edward Harrison Hurley, had trained in Australia as a newspaper typesetter and by 1885 worked in the New South Wales Government Printing Office. Like many other Australians, Edward Hurley came from England and was born in Lancashire, although the family appear to have been Irish-Catholic in origin.

Frank Hurley with his cinematograph apparatus on South Georgia in 1917. He returned there after his rescue from Elephant Island in 1916 in order to fill gaps in his photographic record of the Endurance expedition.

*F*rank Hurley's hometown: "Sydney Harbour Bridge from Circular Quay," c. 1940. This gelatin silver photograph is an example of Hurley's composite images—the clouds were added to produce the right effect.

The family of Frank's mother, Margaret Bouffier, were vintners from Alsace-Lorraine who had immigrated to Cessnock, a mining area in rural New South Wales. The Hurley family appear not to have made much of their Irish origins nor to have been active Catholics. Hurley senior was articulate and was active in union affairs, serving terms as secretary of the New South Wales Typographer's Association, and he had ambitions that Frank might go beyond him to rise further into the professions.

As a boy peering out his attic window on torpid evenings, Frank Hurley dreamed of adventures at sea or beyond the distant Blue Mountains to the west of Sydney rather than of upward mobility. School did not appeal and he did not attend regularly. He was not unusual in this, for, although schooling was compulsory in Australia in the 1880s, absence was common, and most children left at age 13 or 14 to enter the workforce. Frank Hurley probably picked up his thirst for adventure from children's editions of poems and novels that were popular at that time. These stories mixed romanticism with tales of the courage, honor, and self-sacrifice that were required of those fortunate enough to be part of the British Empire. Frank grew up to be not unlike a typical hero of these

"*Power and Speed,*"
c. 1910; a plate from
The Lone Hand,
January 2, 1911.

romantic tales, being big, strong, and good-looking with bright blue eyes and a full head of dark, curly hair. He also had a plucky manner, determined spirit, and the gift of the gab—perhaps inherited from his Irish forebears.

One day in 1898, as he told the story later, fearing the consequences of one of his regular truanting escapades, young Frank quit his school and hopped aboard a freight train to the mountains. After several adventures he ended up in the mining town of Lithgow some 85 miles (140 km) west of Sydney, where he quickly found work as an assistant fitter in the ironworks. Never the complete rebel, Hurley immediately wrote to his parents and received their blessing to stay on. Frank enjoyed the factory work and, at some point, the city boy was also introduced to the pleasures of bushwalking, and possibly amateur photography as well. As he was later to recall in his book *Argonauts of the South*, Hurley at this time in his life kept a firm hold on his father's favorite motto, "I'll find a way or make it"—a line from a rousing poem of the day. He later matched this with a motto of his own, inspired by Marcus Aurelius: "Unless you're beat, you're bound to win."

THE MAGIC OF PHOTOGRAPHY

After a couple of years in Lithgow, Hurley returned to Sydney with a vague plan to go to sea as an engineer. While doing a variety of jobs he undertook technical training courses at night.

Probably around 1904, while employed by the Telegraph Department and learning electrical instrument work, Frank was introduced to the magic of making photographs. Later, he wrote in a diary "From the time I first gazed wonderingly at the miracle of chemical reaction on the latent image during the process of development, I knew I had found my real work, and a key, could I but become its master, that would perhaps unlock the portals of the undiscovered World."

Near mystical conversions like this were common around the turn of the twentieth century when do-it-yourself photography was booming and the postcard craze was underway, bringing the magical results of photography into every home.

Hurley took a lot of time and trouble to seek out people who could help him learn the techniques of photography. His closest friend was a young man of his own age, Henri Mallard, the Australian-born child of French parents who worked at Harrington's Pty. Ltd, a large supplier of photographic materials and equipment in Sydney. Mallard had taken up photography in about 1904, and the two young enthusiasts spent their weekends on excursions and developing their photographs in a darkroom Hurley installed at home in Glebe.

Frank's first published picture, a seascape, appeared in the *Australasian Photo-Review* on June 21, 1905. He then went on to take a series of close-up images of waves breaking against cliffs, a hard subject to capture with the slow speed emulsions of the day and a hazardous one at any time. Over the next few years Hurley became known for dramatic photographs that involved risk and daring as well as technical challenges.

THE NEW PROFESSION

Hurley's path from amateur to professional was rapid. The postcard business was exploding around Sydney, and in 1908 he asked for financial help from his parents and went into partnership with card producer Henry Cave, for whom he may already have worked as an employee. The next few years were filled with long hours of work, filling orders, and creating ever more novelties to tempt a saturated market. By 1910, the company's Power & Speed series were best-sellers. Cave and Hurley cards were typically dramatic, with subjects silhouetted against twilight scenes, sunsets, or the bright lights of the city at night. Some of the cards were hand-colored.

"*S*ydney Post Office by Night from Barrack Street," a Cave and Hurley color postcard with color dyes, c. 1908.

A personal view of these days is reflected in articles he wrote regaling readers of Australian magazines with stories of his exploits to get pictures of fierce surf or of trains bursting out of tunnels swathed in steam (while losing several cameras in the process). To accompany one such article, in *The Lone Hand*, January 2, 1911, five dramatic train pictures were reproduced. Telling the story of how he got his pictures was always an important part of Hurley's lectures and interviews, reflecting his strong sense of showmanship.

By now Hurley was a fully professional photographer, well enough respected to be delivering talks to the New South Wales Photographic Society on such technical challenges as photography at night and combination printing. In 1910 he was a founder member of the Ashfield Camera Club with Henri Mallard and another friend, Norman Deck, and held a one-man show at the Kodak showroom in the same year. In 1911 he was on the committee of the well-established New South Wales Photographic Society's big interstate Salon, demonstrating that in only five years he had risen from one of thousands of amateurs to become their teacher and judge.

Hurley's work at this time resembled that of his Pictorialist contemporaries, although his images tended to be more dramatic. Pictorialism was an international style, involving soft atmospheric lighting and low-angle

"The Last Break, Sydney," a carbon photograph dating from 1905–10, when Hurley was overcoming the technical challenges of photographing dramatic, action-filled scenes.

compositions, shared by "art" photographers since the 1890s. Hurley made a few photographs that followed Australian pictorialists' fondness for soft-focus images in the style of the Impressionistic "nocturnes" painted by the American painter James McNeill Whistler, but his work in the style of the "fuzzy-wuzzies," as the art photographers were called, was limited. Although he adopted the dramatic lighting effects and "story" elements of Pictorialism, his greater debt was to the methods used in creating commercial postcard views, which involved an arsenal of tricks for improving the printed image by adding, subtracting, or heightening details, tones, and effects.

The postcard trade itself, like the growing use of photographs in newspapers and magazines in the first decade of the twentieth century, was a direct response to what was popular with the public. Cards either sold in tens of thousands, or were duds. Original print and photogravure postcard prints were the last major phase of the late nineteenth century "views" trade, in which hundreds of thousands of finely detailed and majestic albumen prints had been sold in Australia alone to be put in albums as mementos and testimonials to colonial progress. Illustrated papers and magazines took over from cards as the most popular form of photographic reproduction even before World War One. The proliferation of these photographs also increased the competition and therefore the need to create attention-grabbing images.

RECOVERING FROM ADVERSITY

Hurley must have felt pleased with his situation by 1910, but in this year the postcard business in Australia suddenly fell into sharp recession. Perhaps because of business woes, his partner Henry Cave became ill and left the business. Hurley was forced to fire his staff and relocate to smaller rooms, but was still left with serious debts to both the Kodak dealership and to Harrington's for supplies.

He also missed the support of his father, who had died prematurely in 1907. Perhaps thinking about him, Hurley described in *Argonauts of the South* how, at a particularly bad time, when he was feeling overwhelmed by his misfortune, he was climbing the stairs to his premises one evening and saw "a silvery beam that shone through a window and flooded the stairway with light." It was a scene worthy of a movie script but also a clue to the meanings he saw in the cloudbursts and beams of light which were to figure so much in his work. He felt a new burst of energy, inspiring him to carry on and "turn the corner"—which, in fact, he did, for soon after, he was off to the Antarctic as the official expedition photographer.

THE ANTARCTIC

This next phase in Frank Hurley's life came about when he met the great Antarctic explorer, Dr. Douglas Mawson. At that time, English-born Mawson was head of the geology department at the university in Adelaide, South Australia, and was paying a brief visit to Sydney. He was there to make preparations for the first Australian scientific expedition to the Antarctic, and to meet Professor T. Edgeworth David, his former professor and companion on the British Antarctic Expedition of 1907–9 in the *Nimrod* under Shackleton. Mawson, David, and their companions had already taken photographs in the Antarctic but Professor David, who was especially skilled in stereophotography, was urging that the expedition should employ a professional photographer.

Hurley made sure he was one of the candidates for the position. Such was his enthusiasm, that rather than

The Mawson expedition established Hurley's reputation as an Antarctic photographer. Shown here is a view of the face of the Neumeyer glacier on South Georgia island, taken on a later expedition.

"Royal Penguins on Nugget's Beach, Macquarie Island, 1911." This carbon photograph was taken on the Mawson Expedition, 1911–14. The remains of the sealing ketch Gratitude, wrecked in 1898, can be seen in the background. The beach was used by seal and whale hunters and there was a penguin oil refinery nearby.

"Out in the Blizzard, Winter Quarters, Main Base, Cape Denison, Adélie Land, 1912." Another carbon photograph taken on the Mawson Expedition, 1911–14. The men are cutting ice blocks for their domestic water supplies.

relying on a brief meeting at the Central railway station in Sydney, he arranged to join Dr. Mawson in his train carriage as he was departing for Melbourne and traveled with him, talking for about two hours, until they reached the stop at Moss Vale. Two days later he was delighted to receive a cable from Adelaide saying "You are accepted." Mawson later said he interpreted Hurley's little stunt as initiative and that this earned him the position as much as his evident technical skills and fitness.

Mawson was deliberately choosing young, fit Australians and New Zealanders for the scientific positions as well as for the crew on his expedition. Hurley's friend Henri Mallard later revealed that he had been first choice for the position but had declined. He put Hurley's name forward instead and then arranged with Harrington's and Kodak to write off Hurley's debts. Kodak took over Hurley's premises as a same-day printing service and Professor David gave Hurley his stereocamera.

Mallard said later that he had had one more favor to perform for Hurley at this time—ensuring that Frank learned how to use a movie camera as quickly as possible. The two of them went out on to the streets to practice, and then developed the film. Coming out of the darkroom having been staring at the frames as they were being developed, Frank said with a sense of wonder, "Look Mal, every one a perfect picture." Hurley himself claimed

in 1927 that his cinematography actually began in 1910 with footage of the Burrinjuck Dam in New South Wales. Be that as it may, Frank Hurley, still only in his mid-twenties, was now poised to start his life as an adventurer, equipped as both a still and cine photographer.

Mawson signed Hurley for a fee of £300 per year plus the promise of using the best cameras available in Australia at the time. Kodak in Sydney was the obvious choice to supply the equipment. On December 2, 1911, Mawson and his team set sail from Hobart, Tasmania, aboard the *Aurora*. Hurley's passion for photography was not always to his companions' advantage, and he managed to complicate what was supposed to be a brief visit to Macquarie Island—where the expedition left a small party and equipment—by delaying proceedings so that he could get a series of pictures of the wildlife on the island.

The journey south was difficult, with the ship having to deal with pack-ice. After two weeks of icy encounters, the *Aurora* found safe haven on Adélie Land in a bay that Mawson chose to call Commonwealth Bay. The *Aurora* then moved on to West Base, 960 miles (1600 km) along the coast, where the party camped at the Winter Quarters in two wooden huts they had built. Hurley's photographic and technical skills were now being constantly put to

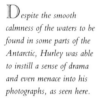

Despite the smooth calmness of the waters to be found in some parts of the Antarctic, Hurley was able to instill a sense of drama and even menace into his photographs, as seen here.

That the beauty of the Antarctic affected Hurley deeply was apparent in his photography. The "dazzling luminosity" that he described in his diary is a result of the reflection of light from the sun, high above the mountains.

the test under extreme conditions. His skills as a fitter and electrician were challenged to their limits, and his talents in the Australian tradition of "making do" were amply demonstrated on many occasions.

On the Mawson expedition Hurley also honed his writing skills, keeping meticulously precise records of everything he did. These records, enlivened by his flair for imagery, would be invaluable to him in the future.

After the winter was over, Mawson waited until late spring to send out a number of small expeditions. One of these involved Hurley, who was selected not only for his photographic skills but also—perhaps even more importantly—for his positive attitude, energy, and strength. His spirit was soon tested. On November 10, 1912, Mawson sent a team consisting of Robert Bage, an engineer and the team leader, New Zealander Eric Webb, the expedition magnetician, and Hurley to take sledges over the Antarctic Plateau to reach the South Magnetic Pole and make scientific readings there. The team worked hard through all sorts of conditions, but found it impossible to complete the journey. On December 21, while still 48 miles (80 km) from the Pole, they turned back. The weather conditions and their situation both deteriorated until it was clear that their lives were in danger. However, when all seemed lost, the weather suddenly cleared and they found themselves looking at the sea and Commonwealth Bay.

Hurley records how, at the darkest moment, "A strange feeling came over me, infinitely comforting. Some indefinable force seemed to be beside me and guiding me on. In a state of high exaltation I knew we were going to win through. Our jaded bodies, still and frostbitten, rebelled, but WILL won." Although Frank Hurley was not a religious man, and was skeptical of much of the Church's teaching, he commented later that the Antarctic experience certainly tended to instill faith.

As 1913 progressed and the time to return to Australia before the onset of the winter blizzards came closer, work began to ready the *Aurora* for departure. While most of the other small expedition teams returned to Commonwealth Bay in good time, Mawson and his team did not. As the pack-ice closed in, the decision was taken to set sail, leaving a small team to wait for Mawson. In fact, Mawson's companions, British naval lieutenant B. E. S. Ninnis and the Swiss Dr. Xavier Mertz, both of whom had signed on as dog handlers, had perished, and Mawson himself only narrowly escaped death because he managed to find a food depot together with directions left by Hurley and one of the search teams that had been looking for him. He returned alone and very ill, having poisoned himself by eating the livers of the dogs. Mawson and the expedition members who had waited for him had to spend another winter awaiting the return of the *Aurora*.

NEW-FOUND FAME

When Hurley returned to Hobart from the Antarctic in early 1913, he found himself a celebrity, as both an adventurer and a photographer. Once back in Sydney, he worked long hours putting together a film and accompanying lectures to raise finances to assist the *Aurora*'s return for Mawson. *Home of the Blizzard* premiered in Sydney later that year. Hurley carefully honed his lecturing style so that he could give a polished performance when providing screen-side commentaries for the film or his lantern slides, some of which were in color, having been made from Paget Colour Plates.

Hurley was on board when the *Aurora* returned to Antarctica on November 16, 1913 to collect Mawson. He made good use of this second visit, spending 10 days at Adélie Land photographing flora and fauna. With Mawson on board, the *Aurora* returned to Australia, this time to Adelaide where Mawson received a hero's welcome. During its time in the Antarctic, Mawson's expedition had charted 2000 miles (3219 km) of coastline, and the knighthood that was bestowed on him soon afterward seemed well-deserved.

With Mawson's Antarctic expedition concluded, Hurley found himself unemployed and with little stock with which to advance his career as all the images he had taken belonged to the expedition by contract. But once again, luck shone on him and a colleague came to his rescue. Francis Birtles, a pioneer of arduous overland motoring, a roving freelance reporter and a cinematographer, approached Hurley to join him on a motor car journey to the far north of Australia. This was, to most Australians, a largely unfamiliar region that formed the "bush" and "outback," where the roads hadn't improved since they were made in the late nineteenth century. Birtles was skilled at promoting his endeavors and was able to gain the support of newspapers to pay for the journey. He also gained a commission from Australasian Films Ltd (later Cinesound) to film the Aboriginal people and outback stations.

The pair left in style from the Sydney Showgrounds on April 14, 1914 on a journey that would take them through thousands of miles of tropical Queensland and the Northern Territory. They returned in August to a welcome in central Sydney's Martin Place. In 1915, Birtles released the commissioned film *Into Australia's Unknown*. Hurley retained many negatives of strikingly beautiful images, especially of Aboriginal life, and used these many times throughout his later exhibitions and publications.

"Playmates—Native Child and Puppy, Northern Queensland." A carbon photograph taken in 1914 during the overland motoring expedition with Francis Birtles.

Hurley with his cinematograph apparatus under Endurance's *bow on September 1, 1915, when he took a group portrait and cinematograph film of the crew.*

ENDURANCE—SAFE RETURN DOUBTFUL

There is a story, almost certainly apocryphal, for the ad has never been found, that the following advertisement appeared in a London newspaper in 1913:

"Men wanted: for hazardous journey. Small wages, bitter cold, long months of complete darkness, constant danger, safe return doubtful. Honour and recognition in case of success."

Couched in full "Boy's Own" style, the advertisement was supposed to have been the work of the explorer Sir Ernest Shackleton, who was seeking to recruit members for his Imperial Trans-Antarctic Expedition, with which he planned to fulfill his dream of being the first to cross the Antarctic ice cap on foot.

In fact, Sir Ernest did not have to advertise his expedition. The simple announcement that he was planning the expedition attracted an overwhelming response, including, it seems, an application from Hurley, though Hurley himself was later to tell a different story to account for how he came to join Shackleton's expedition. He said that Shackleton's backers insisted that he contact and appoint him as the expedition photographer because they were aware of the critical role his films and stills had played in recouping the costs of Mawson's expedition. This is not at all unlikely, in that there was also the precedent set by the significant part played by Herbert Ponting's photography in selling the story of Scott's polar journey.

In Hurley's version of his recruitment to the expedition, he was camped one evening with Francis Birtles miles from anywhere in Queensland, when suddenly an Aboriginal runner appeared with a cable from Shackleton and then ran back the long distance to the Burketown telegraph station to deliver his acceptance. Birtles then drove Hurley all the way back to Sydney.

War had been declared in Europe on August 4 and Hurley sailed from Sydney on one of the last ships to cross the Pacific Ocean to join the *Endurance* and its crew in Buenos Aires, arriving there at the same time as Shackleton. The two men met for the first time in Buenos Aires in mid-October 1914. Originally, Hurley had been hired on a salary basis, with no rights in the pictures. However, by the time the *Endurance* departed Buenos Aires for South Georgia, Hurley had renegotiated his contract to include a 25 percent share in the motion picture rights.

Although Hurley left Sydney for South America and the Antarctic after war was declared in Europe, he did not miss taking part in the Great War. He took this Paget Colour transparency of an Australian Light Horseman picking anemones in Belah, Palestine, in 1917.

What followed became one of the most famous adventure stories of all time, with the expedition's course changing irrevocably when the ship became locked in pack-ice in January 1915.

During the months on the floating ice, Hurley had relatively little opportunity for photography due to the bad weather. However, on August 27, he did manage to capture the now-famous flash photographs of the imprisoned *Endurance*. During this period he also carried out a number of successful experiments in color photography. In mid-October 1915, when the ship was finally crushed, Hurley spent three days on the ice with his movie camera waiting for the end. It came quickly, but not so quickly that Hurley missed getting some extraordinary film footage.

When the expedition members abandoned the ship, Hurley was told to leave behind all film, equipment, and even his exposed plates. Ignoring Shackleton's orders, Hurley managed to retrieve the glass plates and film from the mushy ice water inside the shipwreck. Shackleton caught him doing this, but a compromise was reached and Hurley saved some glass plate negatives, the already developed cinema film, one small Kodak camera, and three rolls of unexposed film. He smashed and left behind about 400 glass plates.

Hurley and most of the crew were eventually rescued from Elephant Island following Shackleton's heroic voyage to South Georgia in the *James Caird*, one of *Endurance*'s lifeboats. At the time, Shackleton's 800-mile (1280-km) voyage captured the public imagination more than anything else about the expedition.

LONDON

Hurley arrived in London from South America on November 11, 1916. It was Hurley's first visit to Great Britain, and he found the atmosphere depressing, the slow pace of the war in Europe and its huge death toll casting a gloomy pall over the nation.

On December 5, 1916, several of Hurley's photographs were used to illustrate an article in the *Daily Mirror* newspaper that highlighted the heroism involved in the rescue of Shackleton's crew. But Shackleton's agents found they were not able to make the best use of the saved film because there were so many subject gaps, so Hurley organized a return trip to South Georgia to gather more images and footage of birds, animals, and the landscape.

On February 15, 1917, only a few months after his rescue, Hurley set sail once again for South Georgia where, after five weeks' work, he succeeded in taking the photographs and shooting the film footage Shackleton required. He also took 72 Paget Colour Plates. Thanks to Hurley's efforts, the film *In the Grip of the Polar Pack-ice* was an overwhelming success, enabling Shackleton to clear all financial liabilities for the expedition. Hurley was now not only a hero but was also seen as a very valuable asset by both expedition financiers and the media.

During the production of the Antarctic photographs, Hurley began to branch out in his use of "composites." This was a process whereby he inserted animals, clouds, whales, people, even the *Endurance* herself, into selected landscape images to give a better idea of the drama of the occasions. He applied to still photography a mode of production familiar and accepted in cine film—an art expected to be believable and convincing in the context of the subject but not necessarily truthful. When Hurley applied this process to reporting and depicting matters which many people considered sacrosanct, such as exploration and matters of national honor, it came to compromise his reputation as a photographer. He never ascribed to the ideals of documentary truth that became the credo of a later generation of photographers and filmmakers, seemingly caring more about the public reception of his work than about the opinion of his peers.

FROM FLANDERS MUD TO PALESTINE

In 1917, the Great War was in its third year. It was a cold and wet winter, the Allies were not faring well, and the battlefields were clogged with mud. To improve morale, the army was looking for positive propaganda from newspapers and their journalists. Captain Hurley, as he was now called in his capacity as official photographer for the Australian Army, arrived in Flanders in August, joining Lt. (later Sir) Hubert Wilkins AFC, who later became a much-decorated explorer, inventor, and pilot. Both men served in the photographic unit under Captain (Dr.) C. E. W. Bean, the official war historian whose task it was to record and enshrine the involvement of the Australian forces in their first major war.

Bean saw his mission in the long perspective of history, not in terms of the news of the moment. He insisted on the primacy of accurate documentary records. In contrast, Hurley focused on the immediate popular audience and was prepared to use whatever means and esthetic techniques he could to communicate the mud, the bravery, the courage, and the unbelievable situations being experienced by the Australian "diggers." For Hurley, using composites was the way to capture the public imagination, and he maintained that the conditions of modern battle could not be conveyed in one negative.

Hurley's philosophy and method of operation in the field and later in the darkroom clashed badly with those of Captain Bean, who referred to Hurley's composites as "fakes." The official censor also caused Hurley a great deal of frustration, because some of Hurley's work was deemed too realistic for the general public. "Our Boys" were not to be shown in an unpleasant light.

Hurley gained some relief from these frustrations when, on November 9, 1917, he was ordered back to England and then on to the Middle East to join the Palestine campaign. He arrived in December 1917, after the Australian cavalry had been victorious in a number of major battles.

Hurley quickly came to enjoy the relative freedom from creative constraints in the Middle East, and also the relaxed attitude and informality of the Australian troops. The Middle East was not the hell-hole of carnage and mud that was the Western Front. General H. G. Chauvel allowed him the use of a band of Light Horse Cavalry to restage some scenes, even of engagements that had not originally involved those particular troops, and he was in his element in putting together his own form of dramatic tableaux. He also took many Paget Colour Plate photographs, most of which were posed scenes with soldiers, and not battle scenes.

Hurley described Palestine as "more Australian, open air, and expansive... It would be a man's bad luck to be killed here in action," and many soldiers regarded Palestine as a holiday compared with France. However, he was soon restless for action and, on one occasion, took to the air with Captain Ross Smith, who was later to make the first London-to-Sydney flight with his brother Keith.

Hurley did find time to relax and, while in Cairo, he fell in love with a petite raven-haired beauty, Antoinette Thierault-Leighton, a young Anglo-French opera singer. She was the daughter of an Englishman, Lieutenant Leighton, and had grown up in Calcutta. It was clearly a case of love at first sight, for Antoinette and Frank married on April 11, 1918 after a ten-day courtship.

Very little is known of Antoinette Hurley's background or of her life before her marriage—except that she had not learned the art of cooking, for she confessed in a rare interview, given to *Australian Women's Weekly* in 1945, that Frank had taught her to cook—and she left no memoir of her life either before or with Frank. Photographs of her

"The Morning after the First Battle at Passchendaele, Flanders," taken October 9, 1917. This is one of Hurley's "composites"—pictures given drama by the addition of objects and effects not in the original. To this battlefield scene, Hurley added sun and clouds to heighten the dramatic effect of the image. The gelatin silver photograph was printed c. 1960.

show her to have been a very stylish woman, and, in contrast to her down-to-earth husband, she was also sociable and cultured. The newlyweds had only a short time together, spending their honeymoon on the Nile—Frank Hurley's only recorded holiday.

The new Mrs. Hurley had to be left behind in the Middle East when her husband returned to England in May 1918 to organize the photographic section of a major exhibition devoted to the Australian Infantry Force held at the Grafton Galleries in London.

The exhibition included many artworks and 130 photographs, most in the form of beautiful large carbon prints. There were also six composites presented as huge enlargements, and a lantern slide projection show of 124 Paget Colour Plates. The show was a great success with the public and Hurley looked forward to taking it on to Australia.

Unfortunately, when Captain Bean visited the exhibition, he disapproved of it, seeing it as the subordination of propaganda for the war effort by Australian soldiers to the promotion of Hurley's name and images—including images that were not his own.

Although Hurley had spent relatively little time at the front during his war work, he had been there long enough to see the carnage and the appalling devastation—unprecedented in warfare—that modern artillery could cause. Identifying always with the public, Hurley felt no concern about preferring to create moving, persuasive images rather than strictly factual ones.

Captain Bean clearly thought otherwise, and made sure that the planned Australian tour of Hurley's photographs did not take place.

RETURN TO AUSTRALIA

Frustrated at the abandonment of an Australian exhibition, from which he could have expected to benefit financially, Hurley sought alternative paths to a post-war livelihood. Before leaving England he arranged to retain the rights to show three Antarctic expedition films and a British war movie, *The Storming of Zeebrugge*, on his return to Australia. He also managed to obtain permission to make a set of smaller print versions of his exhibition photographs. Although the war was not yet over, Hurley, as a civilian, was free to resign from the army and did so on July 11, 1918.

He left for Australia on August 3, gathering up his wife from the Middle East on the way. Relieved to be free of official shackles, Hurley was looking forward to being together again in his home country with "the best women in the world—my wife and my dear old mater."

Antoinette Thierault-Leighton with Captain Frank Hurley at the time of their marriage, Cairo, April 1918.

"The Author Recording a Concert at Aramia," Papua New Guinea, 1921. *A plate (and caption) from Frank Hurley's book* Pearls and Savages, *published in 1924.*

CIVILIAN LIFE: NEW GUINEA AND INDEPENDENT FILMMAKING

Frank and Antoinette Hurley arrived in Sydney on Armistice Day, 1918. He busied himself setting up home, eventually settling in a large house with spectacular views in the affluent harborside suburb of Vaucluse, befitting his status, if not his income, as an explorer and war photographer. Antoinette gave birth to twins, Antoinette and Adelie, in May 1919. The daring, adventurous young photographer was now well established as a mature family man.

Hurley began showing his films, giving lectures, and making new contacts. He tried to garner popular support through the newspapers and he complained about the red tape that was keeping his London exhibition from an Australian showing. But his efforts were to no avail and he had to be content with exhibiting the smaller prints at the Kodak Gallery and publishing them in magazine articles; the prints were eventually collected in the Mitchell Library, Sydney. His lecture tours took him across the country and, though they were hard work, they helped his bank balance grow steadily.

At this time, Hurley liked to be known as Captain Hurley, perhaps in compensation for what he saw as lack of recognition from the military. Although he lost the battle with bureaucracy, he won a permanent place in the national memory and his images came to represent the Australian national identity that was seen as having been tested and forged in the Great War. His images of the diggers on the field of battle emphasized the value and experience of the troops rather than the generals, and they remain the most popular images of any that came from this important period in Australian history.

NEW ADVENTURES

In 1920 Ross Smith, the pilot Hurley had flown with in Palestine, and his brother Keith, won the prize offered by the Australian Government for the first to fly from England in 30 days. They landed first in Charleville, in northern Queensland, where Hurley teamed up with them to accompany them on the rest of their flight south to Sydney. He used film taken on this leg of the journey as the basis for his film *The Ross Smith Flight*. When he needed to show more of the journey, he did not hesitate to cut in film and images from his former adventures in Northern Australia and in Palestine, and even a few fake scenes of cities made by holding postcards in front of his camera lens.

NEW GUINEA

Hurley was able to go journeying again in December 1920, this time to New Guinea. He had dreamed of going to the hot tropics while marooned on Elephant Island and had hoped some of his Antarctic expedition friends would join him. However, he was the only one keen and fit enough to go.

The journey had mixed aims for Hurley. He had accepted a commission from the Anglican Board of Missions to make a film of their work in New Guinea. The Board paid a flat fee for film and slides, and also supplied transport and accommodation. They also agreed that Hurley could take his own films and photographs while traveling at their expense, and he set out to make a commercial travelogue as well.

After island-hopping around the Torres Strait, and visiting missions along the coast of Papua and the Opi River, he fulfilled his contractual obligations, although he was not enthusiastic about the missionaries or the natives he met. His next destination was Yule Island, off the coast near Port Moresby. From there he trekked into the highlands and seemed to enjoy this the more he moved away from the coastal peoples. Besides filming the people and their land, he also made sound recordings of the tribesmen's songs and dialect.

When the Anglican Board of Missions received its footage, later to be released as *The Heart of New Guinea*, they found that the film was more of a travelogue than they had expected, and had too little emphasis on the good works of the faithful missionaries. Although the Board was disappointed, the film was a success with the public, and Hurley's popularity remained high.

Despite the arrival of another daughter, Yvonne, born while Hurley was on his way back from the New Guinea highlands, he showed no sign of sitting quietly at home in Sydney resting on his laurels. He held an exhibition of his Papua New Guinea photographs at the Kodak Gallery in December 1921, where his old friend Henri Mallard was now the manager. In 1922 he released his own part-travelogue, part-ethnographic film, *Pearls and Savages*. At the same time, he began looking at the Australian landscape, visiting the Blue Mountains, and hiking with his old friend Harry Phillips, a photographer with whom he shared a love of the mountains and clouds.

The financial success of *Pearls and Savages* enabled Hurley to organize another expedition into Papua, this time on his own terms. He formed a company called World Picture Exploration, with the specific aim of making travel films. With backing from Kodak, the *Sun* newspaper, and a Sydney businessman called Lebbeus Hordern, who supplied two airplanes, Hurley made ready for this new set of challenges. Keen that the expedition should be seen as scientific, he learned to use the new Marconi radio transmitting devices to keep in touch with the outside world.

Hurley used the footage acquired on the Papua trip to update his first version of *Pearls and Savages* and also made a new film, *With the Headhunters of Unknown Papua*. This was also a popular success and received lavish praise from the *Sun*, although this may have been a little exaggerated by the *Sun's* desire to protect its investment. There was criticism from some quarters of the manner in which certain specimens had been collected by the Australian Museum representative on the team, with allegations that material was taken without permission.

TOURING A WIDER WORLD

Hurley was now setting his sights on much wider horizons. The Papua material having been well used in Australia, Hurley made a visit to America, touring the country giving a series of illustrated lectures and film screenings. A notable achievement of the tour was the taking up of Hurley's story by the New York publisher George Putnam's Sons. In 1924 Putnam published a handsome and beautifully illustrated book by Hurley, *Pearls and Savages*, which was such a great success that they published a second book, *Argonauts of the South*, which was equally successful. Both books were translated into several languages.

After America, Hurley went to England and took the film *Pearls and Savages* on a successful tour before selling it to a German company for £1,500—a considerable sum in those days.

His next venture was not so successful, although it started out well. Hurley gained support for his idea of making his now-characteristic style of feature films from the Australian-born British film magnate Sir Oswald Stoll, and set himself up as an independent film studio. Unfortunately, he was refused permission to film again in Papua, because the authorities there did not wish to support the making of a film likely to show a controversial relationship between the indigenous people and Europeans: Hurley's films tended toward a "brave and noble explorers" and "head hunting savages" view of life.

Despite this setback, Hurley made two feature films in 1926. *The Jungle Woman*, a melodramatic view of race relations, was shot in Dutch New Guinea, and *Hound of the Deep* was shot on Thursday Island. While these films were relatively popular in Australia, mainly because of Hurley's own reputation, they were not generally well received, their naïve and simplistic approach to relationships between the main characters coming in for some criticism. In 1927 Hurley sold a large number of his New Guinea negatives to the Australian Museum in Sydney, suggesting that he planned no further projects with indigenous people. Nevertheless, his films retain an important place in Australian film history.

Hurley now found himself occupied in various kinds of work connected with photography, including acting as picture editor for the *Sun* in Sydney in 1927 and, shortly afterward, spending time in England working as a cameraman in the film studios in Bushey, near London. Although there is no specific supporting evidence, it seems as if this energetic, highly-focused and adventurous man was somewhat dissatisfied with his lot at this time.

All changed when he heard from Douglas Mawson that another Antarctic expedition was being planned. Hurley equipped himself quickly and headed out to join Mawson on the British, Australian, and New Zealand Research Expedition (BANZARE), arranged to explore and research Australian sovereignty over a part of the

Frank Hurley with his BANZARE camera—"trusty friends in adventure"—on the deck of the Discovery, on his way back to Australia after his fourth voyage of exploration to Antarctica. This gelatin silver photograph was taken during the BANZARE Expedition, 1929–30.

Antarctica continent. There were two BANZARE expeditions, both of which resulted in new footage for Hurley, despite the captain's unwillingness to allow what Hurley considered to be sufficient filming time. Even so, Hurley's film, *Southward Ho!*, which he made with Mawson, was another success when it was released in 1930. A later film based on the second expedition and released in 1931 was the first Australian full-length feature film to have music, commentary, and other sound effects.

CINESOUND AND "CAP"

The next eight years saw a fundamental change of lifestyle for Hurley. In 1931, he accepted a salaried position with Cinesound, a subsidiary of Greater Union Theatres. This was an opportune move, given that Australia was suffering severely during the Depression. Three documentary films followed in quick succession: *Jewel of the Pacific*, about Lord Howe Island; *Symphony in Steel*, about the building of the Sydney Harbour Bridge; and *Fire Guardians*, about the work of the fire brigades. All were well received.

At this time, his work also featured prominently in publications issued during the 150th anniversary of European settlement in Australia in 1938, for which he also made the Cinesound documentary *A Nation is Built*. Hurley then joined the team making the second "talkie" in Australia, *The Squatter's Daughter*, which was made to follow up on the success of the first Australian-made "talkie," *On Our Selection*. "Cap," as he was now known at Cinesound, proved his value many times over in brokering deals with locals, and because of his enthusiasm for getting the perfect picture, despite the number of times it required putting himself, and sometimes others, in some danger to obtain it.

In 1936, following success with several documentary films on the power industry, Hurley was placed in charge of a new industrial film department that made commissioned films for corporations and industrial organizations. Here, he was in his element and his perfectionism did not conflict with the ever more elaborate and fast-paced films being made by the company. Work on other Cinesound films followed, including work in 1939 as an outdoor cameraman for Charles Chauvel's World War One epic, *Forty Thousand Horsemen*. For this film Hurley introduced a sunken trench which the horses had to jump over as they were filmed by cameramen below. The rush and excitement of these sequences in the film remain a classic moment in film history.

In mid-life, Frank Hurley was relatively settled, with a good social position and a happy family life in comfortable, even gracious homes, where nannies looked after the children, who now included a son, Frank Jr., born in 1923, and where servants took much of the burden of housekeeping off Antoinette Hurley. From this assured home life, Hurley would sally forth to work, with all his dedication and staying power still clearly in force. He was known for arriving early on the set, remaining attached to his equipment all day, staying formally dressed, and saying little. He would edit his own work to remove less-than-perfect images and often would be the last to leave the set or studio at night. He would also return to retake footage if he was not completely satisfied.

He was no longer remembered for the team spirit that had made him such a vital part of Shackleton's expedition, although he was still humorous and quick-witted with those he knew well or who were important to him. He was rigid in his quest for perfection and unresponsive to the post-war needs of the commercial film and newsreel studio. Despite the difficulties he experienced with Cinesound and they with his methods, his name still meant a great deal to the public, and his employers respected his status and abilities.

BACK TO THE FRONT: WORLD WAR TWO

When Australia declared war in October 1939, Frank Hurley, to his own acute surprise and disappointment, was not asked to take an active role. His efforts to be posted were rebuffed and it is possible that his applications were blocked because, at 54, he was seen as being too old for any sort of "active service." It may also be that he had at least one powerful opponent in the Department of Information, a lingering effect, perhaps, of Charles Bean's condemnation of his World War One "fakes."

Later in the year, the Prime Minister's Office added further insult to the original injury by appointing 23-year-old George Silk, an unknown and technically "amateur" photographer from New Zealand, as a war photographer. Silk won his appointment on the basis of one portfolio of dynamic sailing and skiing pictures taken with a miniature 35mm camera, rather than the larger format used by conventional news reporters. Damien Parer, a young Australian with a passionate interest in the new documentary approach to film, was also appointed.

Damien Parer, Frank Hurley (rear), Maslyn Williams, and George Silk (front) in the Middle East, c. 1941. Gelatin silver photograph.

Hurley was determined to go to war again, and thought he had found a way when he was appointed to the national broadcast radio, the ABC, as a reporter. But he did not make it past Perth in Western Australia. Things changed after Sir Henry Gullett, head of the Department of Information, was killed in a plane crash near Canberra. His replacement was Sir Keith Murdoch who knew Hurley and valued his experience. In August 1940, Hurley was given an acting major's rank and salary and was appointed to oversee the Official Cinematographic and Photographic Unit in the Middle East. He would be in charge of the "young Turks," Parer, Silk, Ron Maslyn Williams, a reporter and cameraman, and Alan Anderson, a sound engineer. Hurley's brief was to represent the Commonwealth but also the news interests of Cinesound and Fox.

He was soon in the thick of the action, following the British and Imperial forces during their North Africa offensive against the Italians in December 1940. As each battle progressed, the unit would have to scamper back to Cairo to develop and print exposed film and to pick up new film. This return journey became more difficult as the front moved farther out, so that Hurley was soon fed up with so much sand, dust, and khaki. The photographic unit was next moved to Syria, which Hurley found a more pleasing landscape than the desert. He was in the wrong zone to capture the action during the June 1941 Syrian Campaign, however, and was annoyed because both George Silk and Damien Parer obtained good photographs for the news.

The man who had been the buoyant team member on the Antarctic voyages is remembered as a loner in World War Two. While there was much socializing amongst the unit, Hurley rarely joined the others for a meal let alone any other social events. Rather, he tended to monitor the younger men and worry about their night life, and he once recorded in his diary that he felt great satisfaction at a Christmas Day spent developing and attending to chores. In fact, it seems that Hurley got on well enough with Parer, who was a devout Catholic, but Silk, whose forté was action photography, and who was both ambitious and determined, disdained not only Frank Hurley's personality, but also his "perfect," but static images.

In December 1941, the Japanese changed the focus of the war for Australia when they bombed Pearl Harbor and began threatening the islands of the Pacific. This brought the war much closer to Australia's own shores. Some Australian troops were withdrawn from the Middle East, along with most of the photographic unit. Silk and Parer went on to make their most famous work in New Guinea, while Hurley stayed with the Ninth Australian Division in North Africa and the Middle East.

He carried on making small featurettes and travelogues, shot away from the action, which he understood to be his brief, and he scorned "slap-up newsreel stuff," carefully editing all his footage and rejecting anything that was blurred or scratched or not well composed. Unlike the younger photographers, Hurley was not inclined to chase the action with smaller cameras. Neither the Department of Information nor the two newsreel companies shared this view and became more and more irritated by the lack of relevance of his featurettes, regardless of how superbly crafted and picturesque they were. Hurley's footage of the Allies' victory at El Alamein in October 1943 was so badly received that little of it was used.

The gap between what his department and the newsreel companies wanted and what Hurley was prepared to produce widened to such an extent that the cost of Hurley's productions could no longer be justified and his withdrawal was being considered—except that no one in Australia knew what to do with this out-of-date but well-respected cinema and still photographer. Fortunately, Hurley solved their problem. His impressive reputation and connections enabled him to resign from the Australian Army and join the British Army, on the pay of a Lieutenant Colonel, as the Director of Features and Propaganda in the Middle East. He was awarded an OBE in 1941 for his war work, making up a little for his lack of decorations in World War One.

Hurley seems to have enjoyed the next forty months, to the end of the War. During this time he oversaw the work of about 50 different film units, as well as having many opportunities to make films and take photographs in one area of the world he loved, the Middle East. Cairo became his second home, but Hurley also spent an enormous amount of time on the road, in the field, and at hands-on work, where he was happiest.

"MAKING A WAY" AFTER THE WAR

Frank Hurley was 61 when he returned to Australia in September 1946, after six years away from family and country. All four children had now married and he was a grandfather. But despite his frugal lifestyle and good pay during the war, he found the family to be in financially desperate straits. Antoinette Hurley had somehow made a mess of the family's finances while her husband had been away. The fine home in Rose Bay, complete with native gardens and lush lawns, had been made the subject of a forced sale, and Antoinette had had to move to a small cottage away from the coast and its superb views.

Undaunted, Hurley set about reestablishing himself and his family. Sensing perhaps that he would not have the independence he had enjoyed with his wartime films, he did not try to find a niche in the rapidly expanding post-war travelogue-documentary or feature film business, although he made one promotional film in 1952, *The Eternal Forest*, for the Australian Paper Manufacturers. He was, however, far from tired. Nor was he unenterprising.

GOING INTO PRINT

Reviving the spirit that characterized him, and claiming "Unless you're beat you're bound to win," Hurley turned to book publishing, an arena in which he felt he could not only serve Australia by promoting the land rather than its war effort, but also make a profit. He regarded Australia as a magnificent witness to the benefits of white settlement and freedom from the racial and social conflicts that had brought war to Europe and the Pacific, and in proof of this he first plumbed the rich resources of his archive.

In 1948, *Shackleton's Argonauts* was published in Sydney, in an edition for a general readership. The book won an Australian book award and was reprinted several times. In the same year, Hurley published *Sydney: A Camera Study*, and in 1949, *The Holy City: A Camera Study of Jerusalem and its Surroundings*. The books, handsome and lavish for the immediate post-war years when rationing still applied and paper was hard to get, were immediate best-sellers. Many continued to be reprinted well into the 1960s. Throughout this period he also continued to make broadcasts on Australian national radio. He had begun broadcasting in 1926, stopping only when he went to war in 1940. Some of his post-war broadcasting involved children's educational programs, which were very popular.

He and Antoinette were soon relocating themselves in better homes, finally settling at Collaroy Plateau, an undeveloped northern Sydney beach area on a large bush acreage with spectacular views, as magnificent as those they had enjoyed at Vaucluse. Sharing a love of gardening, they set to work creating an elaborate garden, and Frank built himself a well-equipped darkroom in the garage.

THE BEST COUNTRY IN THE WORLD

Frank Hurley's next publishing project after the early post-war books involved him in journeys across Australia, state by state, most often with the costs subsidized by state governments and their tourism departments. The result was a continuous flow of superb photographic books on Australia's scenic wonders, cities, rural and heavy industries, as well as native flora. He favored rustling wheat fields and flocks of sheep, all in bright sunshine, and relatively few urban or Aboriginal people appeared in these picturesque, domesticated pastoral scenes. The books were exactly in tune with the market and largely without competition. The scenic view catered to a reviving economy, an intensified relationship with the land experienced by soldiers returning from the distant battle zones, and the post-war drive to attract immigrants.

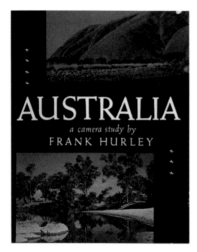

The Australian outback featured prominently on the jacket front of Australia, A Camera Study, *Hurley's 1955 best-seller.*

In 1953 Hurley returned to a craft he knew well from his youth—scenic postcards—and he also entered the world of calendars, producing popular and highly sought-after works year after year. The books in color appear crudely printed by later standards but some of the prints of Australian flora (usually of specimens from his own garden) were brilliant in color fidelity and quality.

Hurley's output became the popular national and international image of Australia for two full decades, and his books were the standard introduction to Australia, found in embassies across the world and on the desks of every newly established tourism office.

In true Hurley style, the Australian photographs were the result of long and arduous journeys to capture that perfect set of pictures. They were taken with a wide view, straight on, without either the low skewed angles favored by Modernist art photography or the atmosphere of early Pictorialism. The compositions were stable, with strong horizontal balance varied by clean vertical elements. Motion was rare and, when they appeared at all, figures posed awkwardly. Also, as old habits die hard, he was not above adding images from former treks into the new photographs when he wanted. For instance, the Palestine sky sometimes found its way into the background of a rural Australian scene! Among his most notable successes of this phase of his richly varied career was his best-seller, *Australia, A Camera Study*, published in 1955.

Hurley was highly active until his death in 1962 at the age of 78. When he realized he was dying, he refused to be coddled and sat upright in his chair all night. At midday the next day, the doctor announced his passing. In 1966, Hurley's daughter Toni collaborated with Frank Legg on a biography of her father, *Once More on my Adventure*.

POSTSCRIPT

Although Hurley's books continued to be reprinted through the 1960s, a new era of coffee-table books overtook his in popularity. American photojournalist Robert Goodman's lavish color book, *The Australians*, published in 1966, became a huge best-seller. It was also a time when Hurley's image of Australia no longer appealed to a younger audience who turned toward more abstract or personalized art and expressions to reflect a cultural renaissance. Hurley had an undisputed position in his lifetime but had missed out on the honors and interest that would start to be awarded to senior Australian cinematographers and photographers still living in the 1980s and 1990s, as the appreciation of photography became part of official culture and museum collections.

Recently, Frank Hurley's name and images have been seen again, both internationally in exhibitions and publications relating to the *Endurance* expedition, and in his homeland, where much work has gone into

This classic photograph epitomizes the lengths that Hurley was prepared to go to to obtain the "perfect" photograph.

biographies and exhibitions concerned with Sir Douglas Mawson's achievements. There is also a growing interest in Hurley's color work. His post-war Australian pictures, too, have found new audiences.

Through recent decades, Hurley's work, held in various archives, has continued to fascinate researchers and curators, and there are available today more publications on Hurley and his work than on any other senior Australian photographer. However, much remains to be seen of his huge output, and he has never been well served by the quality of the reproductions of his work, something this volume attempts to redress.

Some of the modern critiques would no doubt thoroughly bewilder Hurley, but he would be pleased with the renewed national and international interest in his work 75-odd years after he first launched into book publishing in New York in the mid-1920s.

Hurley took to the Antarctic a great quantity of the most up-to-date photographic equipment then available, including equipment for still and cine photography. With such cumbersome equipment, he produced awe-inspiring images, as the panorama in South Georgia, above.

SECTION THREE
PORTFOLIO
SELECTED PHOTOGRAPHS

The deck of the Endurance *showing the arrangement of dog kennels shortly after departing South Georgia. The blankets were a gift of the Scott family at Buenos Aires. Note the pram (the* Nancy Endurance*), a specialized rowboat used by sealers, tied upright in the rigging.*

Most of the Weddell Sea party photographed near Buenos Aires. Top row: Holness, Bakewell. Second row: McNish, James, Wild, Worsley, Stephenson, Hudson, How, Green. Third row: Cheetham, Crean, Hussey, Greenstreet, Shackleton, Sir Daniel Gooch (never considered a permanent member of the expedition; returned to England from South Georgia), Rickenson, Hurley. Front row: Clark, Wordie, Macklin, Marston, McIlroy. Missing are Orde-Lees (who took the photo), Vincent, Kerr, McCarthy, and McLeod. The intriguing possibility exists that Blackborow was stowed away when this plate was exposed.

"The SY Endurance *leaving Buenos Aires on 27 October 1914," reads Hurley's annotation in his* Green Album. *Expedition diaries and newspaper accounts indicate the ship departed on October 26. In his written descriptions, Hurley sometimes confused an image's exposure date with the development-of-image date.*

Perce Blackborow, stowaway, and Mrs. Chippy, McNish's male cat. "[William] Bakewell and Blackborow were sailors on the ship The Golden Gate. *This ship was wrecked on the breakwater at Montevideo. Mr. Bakewell and Blackborow went to Buenos Aires to see if they could find another ship. They saw the* Endurance *and went to see if sailors were needed. Mr. Bakewell was taken on, Blackborow was not as he was too young…"* Blackborow considered Ernest Shackleton to be one of the greatest explorers in history.

Frank Wild enjoying time on deck with some of the dogs during the journey from Buenos Aires to South Georgia.

King Edward Cove, South Georgia island, 1914. The Endurance is the smaller of the two ships at anchor.

Hurley, Worsley (in white sweater), and Greenstreet climbed
Duce Fell on November 13, 1914, carrying Hurley's heavy whole
plate camera and lunch on a sledge. Near the summit, they had
to cut steps with an ice ax and haul the camera up by a rope.
Endurance is anchored in East Cumberland Bay far beneath them.

Endurance *baptizes her bow on the Weddell Sea pack-ice, December 1914.*

Cruising under steam *through loose floes of pack-ice in the Weddell Sea, as seen from the crow's nest.*

"During the day, we had a very gratifying run, passing through vast fields of young ice, or rather recently formed ice in a rapid state of dissipation. The ship cut her way through in noble style, leaving a long wake which could be traced, and remaining open, for a mile or so."

HURLEY DIARY
JANUARY 1, 1915

Endurance *cutting her way through fields of ice*

Reaching for the open ocean—and Vahsel Bucht. While other similar images were captured by Hurley from the same spot, this is the only one of the bunch that was recorded on a 1/1 plate.

"...at 10am we entered long leads of ice-free water in which were drifting some fine bergs of magnificent forms. One, a fine cuniformed mass, 200 feet high, I photographed."

HURLEY DIARY
DECEMBER 21, 1914

"...I fitted up a weather screen on the bridge..." wrote ship's carpenter Harry McNish on December 11, 1914. The following day, McNish "...had breakfast & oiled all round & cleaned tools & made semaphore signal for bridge." This photo was probably exposed on the same day or shortly thereafter.

Exercising the dogs on the ice during a hold-up on January 6, 1915, the first time the dogs had been unchained and out-of-cage for nearly a month.

"Fast to floe & exercise dogs muzzled slipping & several involuntary immersions. Two dogs take a pool of very blue water & brash ice for something to walk on; three others simply fall over the edge. All enjoy exercise immensely."

WORSLEY DIARY
JANUARY 6, 1915

" A *small berg –
with ice blink horizon.
8 January, 69° 28' S,
20° 9' W…" as
recorded by Hurley in
his Green Album.*

*Shackleton examines the
ice ahead of the ship while
Hurley secures the scene on
cinematograph film from a
vantage place aloft.*

*Hurley's camera
captures the icy
solitude of
Antarctic waters*

*A rare bit of open
water encountered on
January 13, 1915
en route to Vahsel Bucht.*

"Hurley the irrepressible … is taking a colour photo of the ship & ice… He is a marvel – with cheerful Australian profanity he perambulates alone aloft & everywhere, in the most dangerous & slippery places he can find, content & happy at all times but cursing so if he can get a good or novel picture. Stands bare [headed] & hair waving in the wind, where we are gloved & helmeted, he snaps his snap or winds his handle turning out curses of delight & pictures of Life by the fathom."

WORSLEY DIARY
JANUARY 24, 1915

The Barrier of Coats Land, estimated to be approximately 100 feet (30.8 m) high. Latitude 72° 10' S, longitude 16° 57' W. Although not evident in the photo, seals and penguins were numerous, the sea changed from a deep blue to light green color, and the ship, unimpeded by bergs, enjoyed the expedition's best run (136 miles/ 218 km) during the day, January 10, 1915.

The ship's rigging cased in rime.

Reginald James noted in his diary on January 25, 1915 that Hurley "got a fine colour picture of Cheetham … with the red ensign & the Australian flag." The following day Orde-Lees recorded that "Hurley has taken some splendid colour photos."

John Vincent mending a net on the deck of the Endurance.

Although Hurley's Green Album *indicates that this photo was taken before the ship was beset, it endures as a classic portrait of the ship—and the ice. Note the slight starboard list in the ship.*

While *this photo could have been taken at nearly any time during the ship's enforced captivity in the ice, the plate was likely to have been exposed shortly before the* Endurance *was beset, when Orde-Lees and Hurley went skiing.*

Life on the ice as Endurance *awaits an opening to the sea*

While *passing these birds on January 12, 1915, but before realizing they were Emperor penguin chicks, Shackleton ordered the* Endurance *turned around and ran her bow up on the floe to investigate what he thought was a new species of Antarctic bird life.*

"Towards midnight of yesterday the ice began to break up & a lead opened only 200 yds. ahead of us. By 10am this broadened to ¼-mile. All sails were therefore set, & with engines at full speed, an attempt is made to break through the ice. For 3 hours we remained fast, the only effect being to wash some ice away astern & clear the rudder. I go 'ashore' & take picture of ship & floe."

HURLEY DIARY
JANUARY 25, 1915

"Hurley was out on the floe photographing the ship but had to return hurriedly as the hummock that we had our stern made fast to by a wire broke off with a piece of the floe attached and we began to swing out away from the floe. This was probably due to having set some sails for the sake of making a good picture, though there was only the lightest of zephyrs blowing."

ORDE-LEES DIARY
JANUARY 14, 1915

Portrait of Tom Crean,
February 7, 1915.
"A … fine character one
of the most reliable men
on the expedition. As his
name suggests he is an
Irishman & a giant at that.
He started as an ordinary
sailor in the navy & was
in Scott's expedition on
HMS Discovery & again
in his last expedition
when, by walking thirty
miles alone to fetch help,
& thereby save the life of
Commander Evans
dangerously ill with scurvy,
he gained the Albert medal
for conspicuous bravery.
His staunch loyalty to the
expedition is worth a lot."

ORDE-LEES DIARY
OCTOBER 10, 1915

Crean retired to his
birthplace, Annascaul,
Ireland, where he
established the South
Pole Inn, which is still
in operation today.

Captain Frank Worsley
at the rear hatch abreast
of his cabin.

Shackleton's cabin,
originally Worsley's,
aboard Endurance.
Shackleton was especially
interested in the men's
"learnings," encouraging
them to borrow and read
the Polar books in his
library, and frequently
questioning them when
the books were returned
or exchanged. McNish
installed the "bogie" and
insulated the cabin in
early March, 1915.

Apparently, this photo was exposed from the deck of the ship. Hurley's description, which is most confusing, simply reads, "A mid-summer sunset with close up view of Endurance frozen in."

The starboard deck of the Endurance, *forward perspective.* "Owing to the fallen temperature – it being -19, a heavy condensation develops on cameras when brought aboard. I have made a cupboard on deck where they may be kept at an even low temperature. Nevertheless, the apparatus needs attention every occasion it is taken out, lubricating with petroleum, etc., especially the Cinematograph. Under these extreme temperatures, the [Kodak] film becomes extremely brittle and loses about 10% of its sensitiveness."

HURLEY DIARY
APRIL 24, 1915

The ice surrounding and overlaying the ship after she was beset

Crean and "his" pups (produced by Sally and Samson): Roger, Toby (back), Nell (front), and Nelson, photographed one month after they were born.

"Further progress southward was blocked by impenetrable pack. January 20, 1915. Taken the day after Endurance was finally 'held up' and where she was eventually frozen in," wrote Frank Hurley in the Green Album.

Crean's pups were born on January 7, 1915. They were captured by cinematograph and plate film on February 7.

Dawn at the close of winter

"Noon. Mid-winters day, 1915," reads Hurley's description of this photo. However romantic that may sound, especially when coupled with this image, June 22 was the darkest day of the year. The photo was undoubtedly taken at another time.

The boom for Clark's net, used for gathering specimens from the ocean bottom, is clearly seen in this distant view of the ship during the spring of 1915.

Frank Hurley, photographer (right). "He always mixed his own chemicals, did all his own developing and printing, colouring, everything. He had his big tanks and enlarger and the rest. His fingernails were always brown because of the chemicals."

Leonard Hussey, meteorologist (right). "He is a Londoner by birth & is continually being chaffed about being a cockney a part which he often acts to perfection. His wit and repartee are exceedingly bright and invariably in the best taste. He is a B.Sc. (Bachelor of Science) of the London University & reckoned very good at his own job. Although no more than 23 years of age he has had previous experience, having been a member of the Welcome expedition to the Sudan under Mr. Welcome of the firm of Burroughs & Welcome. He is a lean joist of unusual merit and it is very pleasant to have music of any kind down here; his [banjo] repertoire is sufficient to prevent his tunes becoming too monotonous… Hussey is one of our smallest members but he makes up in energy what he lacks in stature."

Orde-Lees diary
October 14, 1915

Frank Wild, February 7, 1915 (left). "He acts as Sir Ernest's lieutenant and if he has any orders to give us he gives them in the nicest way, especially if it is instructions to carry out some particularly nasty work such as 'trimming' coal in the bunkers… His competence is his outstanding feature; whatever there is to be done he knows just how to do it and yet he never appears to be dogmatic about it."

Orde-Lees diary
June 13, 1915

George Marston, artist (above). In addition to being a dog driver slated for the transcontinental journey, Marston was in charge of the expedition clothing and invented the tents used after the ship was crushed. Although he lost his art when the crew took to the ice, he continued to sketch and paint, even when reduced to a small sketch book, six tubes of watercolors, and a pencil. His oils and water-colors are among the most enduring representations of the expedition.

Alexander Macklin, surgeon (top, right). "A Scotchman born & bred in the Scilly Isles where his father is one of the leading practitioners. Educated at Plymouth College and Edinburgh University, he held a post in a hospital at Manchester before joining the expedition. Though he gives no indication of it in his voice, he yet has the main Scotch characteristics. Rather quick tempered he is at the same time a thorough sportsman in the best sense … one of our hardest workers, continually out amongst his dogs even in the most inclement weather."

Orde-Lees diary
September 26, 1915

Lieutenant Frank Worsley, R.N.R. (above). "He is a vital spark. His activity and keenness are extraordinary… I am sure he must be invaluable as a helpmate to Sir Ernest… Everyone recognizes his undoubted suitability for the post he holds… I have always found him a sound counsellor & firm friend."

Orde-Lees diary
July 11, 1915

Hubert "Buddha" Hudson, navigating officer (above), with Emperor penguin chicks, January 12, 1915. Considered a widely traveled ladies' man by the Endurance crew, he was also thought a bit "dull." During the boat journey to Elephant Island, Hudson suffered frostbite to his hands, which remained deformed for the rest of his life.

Robert "Bob" Clark, biologist (top, left). "A thorough good sort. He is a footballer of some merit and 'runs' our games for us. He is very hard working, forever skinning penguins … a marine biologist & an all round naturalist of some considerable attainments being a B.Sc…"

ORDE-LEES DIARY
OCTOBER 14, 1915

Reginald James, physicist (above, left). "Jimmy … is a very learned person… Reddish haired with spectacles and inclined to stoutness he is a B.Sc. of Cambridge where he was recently employed as demonstrator in the Cavendish laboratory. His facility with figures is, to me, always surprising."

ORDE-LEES DIARY
JUNE 29, 1915

Thomas Orde-Lees, motor expert, later store-keeper, (above, right). He kept an extensive diary where, among other things, he chronicled others' impressions of himself, to wit, "Lees is inclined to be a little over anxious to please Sir Ernest … and last night Dr. McIlroy 'took him off' cleverly."

ORDE-LEES DIARY
JUNE 7, 1915

James Wordie, geologist (left). "'Jock'… is another true Scotchman from Glasgow. He has a most amiable temperament & a wonderful fund of very dry humour, & a happy knack of 'pulling one's leg' in a quiet sort of way that leaves one more pleased than hurt. He too is a B.Sc. (of Cambridge) having been college mates with James, our physicist. In default of rocks to vent his spleen on 'Jock' has made a great study of glaciology & I have no doubt that with his keen philosophical judgment he will produce a book of great merit upon this interesting & little known subject. Taking him all round he is at once the most inoffensive & one of the most popular of our members. He has no use for cliques, which have unfortunately developed a little and are well known to be the bane of expeditionary life."

ORDE-LEES DIARY
OCTOBER 16, 1915

Sir Ernest Shackleton (right). "Never the lowered banner, never the last endeavour."

Clearing Endurance's *deck of snow during a hold-up on the way south to Vahsel Bucht.*

Beginning to cut ice away from the bow of the Endurance *on February 14, 1915.*

Close-up view of the men at work on the ice beside the ship.

Preparing for a break-out: all hands turned to in the effort to free the ship

Attempting to
break out of the ice,
February 14–15, 1915.
Original negative.

Poling ice away from the
starboard side of the ship,
February 14–15, 1915.

"Alf" Cheetham—
"Cupid on a water
Lilly [sic],"—photographed
(and cinematographed)
during the last attempt
to break out of the ice,
February 14–15, 1915.

Teamwork on the ice:
another view of the attempt
to pole ice away from the
ship's starboard side,
February 14–15, 1915.

Hazardous work:
attempting to free
the Endurance
from the ice

The Endurance *viewed
through the perspective of
a distant pressure ridge.
Hurley titled this photo
"A midwinter glow."*

*Shackleton's final
attempt to release
Endurance from its
"icy grip" in the Weddell
Sea, February 14, 1915.
"…everyone, like a
Trojan, would wielded
a pick, ice chisel, or other
implement. The ship
itself was commissioned
as a battering ram,"
recorded Hurley in
latitude 76° 50' S,
longitude 34° 58' W.*

"At 4pm we had a grand cinema football match with two full teams of eleven a side ... and we had a much needed and capable referee in Dr. Macklin, who, though one of our best players, was unable to play owing to having been bitten rather badly by one of the dogs this morning whilst separating two combatants."

ORDE-LEES DIARY
FEBRUARY 16, 1915

The exposure (left) shows Worsley in goal during the afternoon soccer game, February 16, 1915. Original negative.

Participants in the soccer game held February 16, the day following the last attempted break-out of the ice. "At 4 o'clock we had a grand foot ball match," wrote Reginald James, "11 a side. One team wore a red band on the arm, the other white ... 1–1 but in the second half 'reds' scored the winning goal. Cinematograph took it all in."

JAMES DIARY
FEBRUARY 16, 1915

Hurley credits this photo to January 1, 1915, at latitude 76° S, longitude 35° W. Interestingly, Endurance did not reach that approximate position until January 19—when she was beset.

A distant view through hummocks of the Endurance with men at exercise beside the ship. Spring 1915.

The Endurance *from
afar, most probably taken
the same day Hurley
exposed a similar view
in Paget Colour.*

Pylon Way from aloft—
the path to the lead ahead
of the ship where ice was
cut. The track was laid
out, the large snow cairns
built, and a cable installed
during March 1915,
so that lost explorers
could find their way
home during a blizzard.

Usually titled
"Furthest South" in
expedition literature and
credited by Hurley to
"2nd September," this
photo bears the trademarks
of similar negatives exposed
in mid-February, 1915.

A flashlight study of Hussey's Dine's anemometer blades covered with thick rime. When turning, the anemometer gauged wind velocity.

"Dogloos" around the ship on a day of clear weather, 1915. McNish closed in the stern house during March while Hurley put Hussey's meteorological screen in place about the same time. Blankets were offered to the dogs shortly after the "dogloos" were constructed, but the dogs, treating them as toys, soon tore them to shreds. At the same time, a hole was cut through the ice at the stern of the ship to keep the rudder free and to provide a source of water should a fire erupt on board.

*S*ledging blue ice back to the ship.

"*T*his hand hoisting [of the Hjort Meter net for Clark's samples] is a big undertaking and occupies all available hands. About fifteen of us put the wire over our shoulders; it passes over a pulley on a derrick, and we just tramp away with it. When we get about a quarter of a mile away from the ship the wire is slipped round another pulley, a snatch-block, & we all walk back to the ship with it ... all dressed in motley polar costumes, some with Burberry suits, most of us with reindeer hair finesko boots & all in various head gear, but all muffled up, for it is often cold work, waiting about for orders."

ORDE-LEES DIARY
JUNE 11, 1915

The "Spectre Ship," perhaps Hurley's most enduring photograph of the Endurance. "Hurley has been taking flashlight pictures he has secured some of the best."

McNish diary
June 9, 1915

Original whole plate.

"After three attempts, I succeed in securing flash-light of my team being fed. The charges of flash powder were placed in three shielded receptacles and fired electrically. The dogs were extremely scared, the kennel entrances having to be blocked to keep them out."

Hurley diary
May 29, 1915

During the winter of 1915, all the fit sledging dogs were weighed every week, usually on Thursdays. "I helped Hurley weigh the dogs," noted Reginald James on May 20, 1915, while Frank Worsley recorded the findings:

"My turn to night watch," Hurley later recorded about the small hours of June 30, 1915. "The night watch also arouses his friends, and they sit in quorum around the bogie fire, discoursing in subdued whispers."

Orde-Lees noted that he never got much sleep when Hurley stood night duty—Hurley was boisterous and talked loudly because he was tone deaf.

Usually titled "The night watchman returns…" in popular accounts, Hurley has noted the figure as "Clark returning from winter exercise," in the Green Album. Note the heavy encrustation of rime on every available surface.

Approaching
Endurance *on Pylon*
Way from the lead
ahead, March 1915.

Ice flowers on a lead,
spring 1915.

Shackleton ordered crew members to share duties, as portrayed here in the bi-weekly task of scrubbing the Ritz floor by Wordie, Cheetham, and Macklin. Shackleton himself assisted in laying the linoleum in March 1915.

Hurley and Macklin ensconced in their snug home, the "Billabong," which they shared with McIlroy and Hussey during the winter of 1915. For teetotalers like Hurley, Shackleton provided Carson's chocolates on Saturday evenings when the crew raised the traditional toast to "Sweethearts and Wives."

Midwinter's Day, June 22, 1915, heralding the return of the sun, was celebrated as a holiday. "Dinner at 6-0," noted Harry McNish in his diary, "Roast Pork stewed apples & preserved peas with plum pudding & ... then we had a concert which started at 8-0 & finished at 12 PM with fried onions & ... then we drank the health of our Loved Ones at Home."

Midwinter's Day, 1915. Participants pose in their costumes after the three hour "smoking concert" on June 22 which celebrated the sun's return. Hussey is made up as a black minstrel, complete with banjo. Rickenson is the "flapper." Kerr, outfitted as a ragamuffin, poses with Greenstreet, the elderly roué in a red wig; they sang a duet, "La diddley iddley um." Wild, made up as a small boy who effected a lisp, recited

"The Schooner Hesperus," aided by Hudson costumed as the captain's daughter. Wordie offered a skit of a Scotchman tuning his bagpipes while Clark, in his kilt, rendered a Scottish ballad. McNish, without aid of musical accompaniment, continued with two Scotch dirges. James, a German linguist of accomplishment, gave a fanciful lecture on "the calorie" which took the audience by storm. Marston appeared as a

country farmer singing "Widdicomb Fair," and later rendered a blood-curdling rendition of "Johnny Hall." James McIlroy appeared as the perfumed grisette—his presentation was not reckoned acceptable for polite British society. Dr. Macklin recited topical verses detailing the Endurance's voyage from Plymouth to Buenos Aires, taking advantage of Worsley's excess of zeal during the journey—"We

are His Majesty's Ship Endurance bound for adventure in the far South!" Lees, as Reverend Dr. Bubblinglove, opened the show with a bombastic speech welcoming Shackleton to the concert about to unfold before him. Hurley, who apparently did not dress for the show, read "excellent" verse detailing the troubles encountered by the night watchman.

Playing billiards on a miniature table in the Ritz was one way to pass the icebound hours during the winter of 1915.

"A midwinter morning in the Ritz," reads Hurley's description in the Green Album for this 1915 photo. On the right: Hussey, James, Wordie, Clark. To the left are McNish (who made a cribbage board on February 17–18), Blackborow toting the ice block, and Orde-Lees using Shackleton's typewriter.

"A form of mid-winter madness has manifested itself, all hands being seized with the desire to have their hair removed. It caused much amusement, and luxuriant curls, bald pates and parted crowns soon became akin. We are likely to be cool-headed in the future, if not neuralgic. We resemble a cargo of convicts, and I did not let the opportunity pass of perpetuating photographically this humorous happening."

HURLEY DIARY
MAY 19, 1915

Gramophone concerts were enjoyed each Sunday evening once the ship was beset, but were eventually abandoned because the ice commenced grinding against the ship's side when the music began to play.

Dr. Macklin and
Commander Greenstreet
boiling blubber for the dogs
during the wee hours of
any, and many a polar
night, 1915.

Marine Biologist "Bob"
Clark, captain of the
Afterguard soccer team, in
his lab tweendecks after the
ship was converted to
winter quarters,
February–March 1915.
An expert taxidermist,
Clark often bemused the
men by doing his work on
the crew's dining table, the
evening meal sometimes
laid around a carcass.

"Return of the sun after the long winter darkness," reads the inscription in the SPRI Blue Album, one of several such keepsakes manufactured by Raines & Company.

"Ice breakers, pressure centre, 1st August 1915," wrote Hurley in his Green Album. Often used to illustrate various expedition accounts, this photo is usually titled "Almost overwhelmed."

"In the afternoon Hurley &
I do a 6 mile round with the
camera... I dispose my manly
figure in more or less graceful
poses as an accessory to the
surrounding scenery – a kind
of human meter to gauge the
sublimity of Nature."

WORSLEY DIARY
AUGUST 16, 1915

Rafting ice with the ship in the distance, April 4, 1915. A very typical yet rarely used image of events in the Weddell Sea.

Worsley's "manly figure" illustrates the size of what the Endurance members considered a typical pressure ridge.

"Rafting and tilting." Ice conditions existing in August 1915.

Hacking blue ice from a hummock for use back on board the ship.

Packing ice, collecting specimens, exercising dogs: always plenty of work on the ice

Wordie and Clark investigate the haul from Clark's net. "Clear weather... After breakfast we complete [a] large igloo for the dogs using the starboard side of the ship with an awning stretched sloping down to a wall of petrol cases & an ice wall on the other end."

WORSLEY DIARY
MARCH 21, 1915

Original negative.

"The crew are getting a gangway fitted up on the Starboard side for the dogs going on the floe," wrote Harry McNish on August 18, 1915. On August 25 he simply noted, "leaders and drivers fotoed."

Leonard Hussey often
accompanied Hurley on his
sledge journeys.

"The ice immediately
ahead of the ship.
August 1915" was
Hurley's note for
this photo in his
Green Album.

Lionel Greenstreet photographed with "breath icicles" when exercising with Hurley and his team, September 1915.

Hurley's team with Greenstreet in the rear and Shakespeare in the lead. Directly after the August 1, 1915 break-up of the ice, Hurley and the other dog drivers used small, partially loaded sledges while exercising their teams until distinct tracks were laid out through the myriad of hummocks brought by the dramatic change in the ice.

"Returning from winter exercise," reads Hurley's description in the Green Album. However, the photo shows bright sunlight and was doubtless taken after the dogs were brought back aboard the ship in August 1915.

Harnessing the more experienced dogs for a day's exercise, while "Crean's pups," nearly full grown, wander freely through the pack. Spring 1915.

Judge, a member of George Marston's sledge team, took an immediate dislike to his new mattress when it was offered to him in March 1915, but growled when Macklin tried to remove it.

Considered a wise and friendly dog, and senior member of the pack, he was shot by Wild on August 14 when found to be infested with tape worms, many of them a foot long. Satan, Sandy,

Sooty, and Roy were put down the same day. Copy negative.

Portrait of a dog noted as "Samson" in Hurley's Green Album, *which contains a similar image with the dog's head turned the other direction.*

Lupoid *(far right), named for his wolfish appearance.* "After breakfast the dogs are exercised towards the SE where they get a run 2½ miles clear of cracks. Soldier sights a penguin & takes charge… By the time [Wild] arrives on the scene Soldier & Lupoid have killed the Emperor & are sitting up smothered in blood, Soldier with his usual air of 'done my duty & don't give a damn' but Lupoid wears an aspect of terrible remorse."

WORSLEY DIARY
SEPTEMBER 30, 1915

Hussey and Samson, spring 1915. The nearly full-grown pup is Nell, one of Crean's pups, produced by Sally and Samson.

There was a close relationship between the men and their dog teams

"Samson," reads Hurley's description of this photo in the Green Album. Samson is usually acknowledged to be a large St. Bernard.

Owd Bob.

This Paget Colour Plate
of the ship's rigging
encrusted with rime, "thick
as a man's wrist," may
have been exposed on
September 1, 1915 when
Hurley experimented with
the Paget Colour process.

*D*og teams and their
drivers on break during
exercise while beset
aboard Endurance
in the Weddell Sea,
spring 1915.

Dawn at the close of the Antarctic winter, August 1915, after the disruption with the ice, and the dogs once again aboard the ship.

The deck of the Endurance after a light snowfall. Hussey's meteorological screen was removed from the stern of the ship and placed in the motor boat, left, on October 11, as the crew made preparations for sailing when the ice broke up.

April sunrise, 1915. Note the "rickers" attached to the masts—and wires spread aloft and far afield—for the reception of Morse code signals. "Rig 3 rickers," recorded Frank Worsley on March 29, 1915. "They are 20 feet long & will lift antenna 14 or 15 feet higher than before. Hurley the versatile – one of whose partially abandoned past positions was that of an electrical engineer [orchestrates the making of] 4 long wires on 4 bamboo spreaders each 14 ft. long in such a way that we will have three times the receiving surface of wire that we had leaving South Georgia." As a result of the accumulating weight of the thick rime and the constant maintenance they required, the "rickers" were removed a month later.

Shackleton examines an opening lead in the Weddell Sea, caused by warmer temperatures. Spring 1915.

The men of Endurance *make their mark, albeit short-lived, on the Antarctic world*

The compound and "dogloo" where Sally and her first offspring (Crean's pups) resided while the four pups became accustomed to Antarctic conditions. February 1915.

"My 'observatory' was very picturesque, between two large hummocks & Hurley coming out on a search for a picture was struck with it and took it."

JAMES DIARY
FEBRUARY 16, 1915

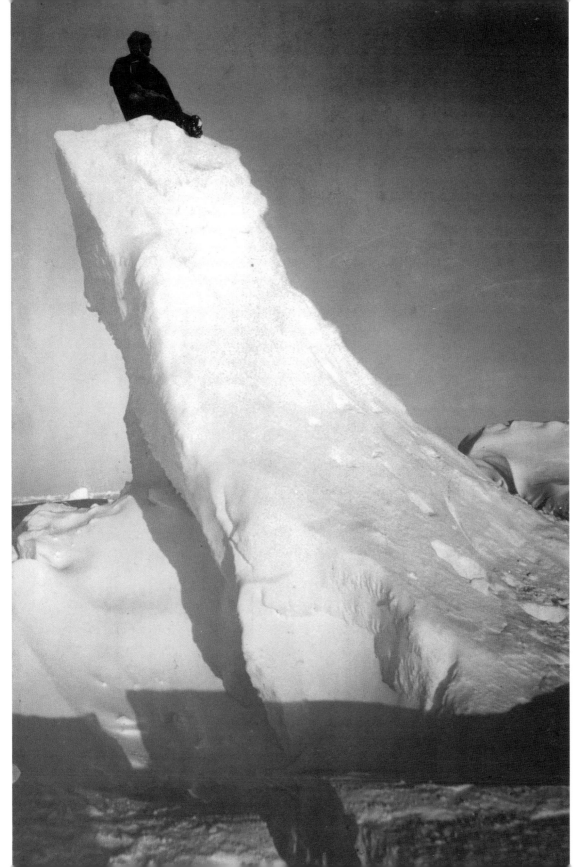

"Hurley went on photographing expedition & got some very good pictures. I was with him. He got an excellent snap of a seal jumping out of a crack on to the floes."

JAMES DIARY
OCTOBER 12, 1915

A favorite rendezvous for the dog teams was the Obelisk. An idea of its proportions can be gained by looking at Worsley, who is pictured atop it.

Hurley with
cinematograph under the
bow of the Endurance,
September 1, 1915.

The crew of the
Endurance,
September 1, 1915.
According to Harry
McNish, Hurley took this
group photo on Wednesday,
September 1, 1915; he
also exposed several yards
of cinematograph film.

About 7:00 p.m. on October 14, 1915, the eve of Hurley's 28th birthday, the ice split with a thunderous crash, causing the crew to rush topside to the slushy deck. The ice had split and freed the ship, allowing an examination of the helm, which was discovered to be twisted from the waterline to the second rudder band. After hoisting the spanker, the ship actually sailed— for a scant 100 yards (91 m)—before coming to rest in a narrow lead blocked ahead by bergs. Endurance was crushed on October 27 in this new location.

Shackleton watching
the floe cracking up
ahead of the ship.

A close-up view of
the ship's bow.

Lantern slide depicting events of October 24, 1915, when the ice attacked the ship, damaging her stern post, and causing a leak. "6.45 ship sustained heavy pressure through having got pushed into a bad angle floes & pressure ridges ... forcing starboard quarter against floe & twisting sternpost starting hidden ends of planking and making ship leak dangerously."

WORSLEY DIARY
OCTOBER 24, 1915

The ship heeled over on her port side.

Endurance *heeled to*
port, stern perspective.

Endurance *in her death*
throes in the Antarctic ice.

A *close-up view of the deck of the* Endurance.

T*he* Endurance *forced out of the floe by heavy pressure, October 18, 1915.*

"The floes are in a state of agitation throughout the day, and in consequence, I had the cinema trained on the ship the whole time. I secured the unique film of the masts collapsing."

HURLEY DIARY
OCTOBER 28, 1915

Due to the severe climatic conditions, Hurley often used his whole plate camera next to his cinematograph apparatus.

Early on the morning of October 28, 1915, after their first night camped on the floe, Shackleton, Wild, and Hurley picked their way through hummocks to the wreck, retrieving several tins of benzine. A fire was kindled at "Dump Camp" and breakfast was cooked for the men. Wild served breakfast to the men in their sleeping bags, later writing they did not fully appreciate the effort that went into preparing or serving the meal. Original nitrate.

The wreck

The wreck of the
Endurance: *a tangle
of spars, masts,
and rigging*

*One of three existing
exposures made by Hurley
on November 1, 1915
before the unsafe mainmast
was cut away, allowing the
men to commence salvage
operations on the wreck.
Copy negative on cut film.*

Hurley's best known and most widely reproduced photograph of the wreck. Original whole plate.

Frank Wild surveys the ship's remains on November 8, 1915, when he, Shackleton, and Hurley paid the last official visit to the wreck.

"The camp," wrote Hurley in his Green Album, *failing to specify exactly which camp. While the setting portrays what seems to be the earliest days of Patience Camp, the image was* captured on a whole glass plate at Ocean Camp, *which was sometimes removed to other floes and otherwise rearranged due to vagaries in the ice.*

An informal group portrait, Ocean Camp, 1915. Shackleton, Wild, and Orde-Lees figure prominently in the photo. Perhaps more eye-catching here are Hurley's boxes of plates, lenses, and other photography equipment stacked neatly beside the door of Shackleton's tent.

"Hurley & Kerr were finishing off the stove all day, working in the big tent. It is a wonderful piece of ingenuity & excellent work considering the paucity of tools."

ORDE-LEES DIARY
NOVEMBER 7, 1915

Ocean Camp shortly
after it was established,
showing Worsley's
observation platform (rear),
Hussey's meteorological
instruments (left), and the
dogs in the foreground.

Panorama of Ocean
Camp showing its location
to the ship, the funnel of
which is just visible on the
skyline, center left.

On December 8, 1915,
their 43rd day on the floe,
the men hauled the refitted
James Caird to a lead
250 yards (228 m) from
Ocean Camp and tested
it in the water (see over).
After the successful
experiment, while replacing
her on the sledge, her

stern was damaged when
the angle of pull was
overridden by the block
and tackle on "shore."
The following day, in
camp, lines were placed on
all the boats to assure their
eventual, safe, hauling-up.

Shackleton's tent under blue skies at Ocean Camp, with the King's flag and ship's burgee flying proudly from a spar. Orde-Lees's skis, Hurley's boxes of photographic equipment, Worsley's observation tower, and the day's drying laundry all figure prominently in the photo.

After the loss of the ship, Hurley, ever inventive, became an aggressive hunter, manufacturer of weighing scales and bilge pumps, and an inveterate stove-builder. On November 26, 1915 he drew this stove (left) in his diary. Reginald James photographed the stove, which acted like a "blast furnace" on November 29, 1915. James's diagram, made the same day, bears an uncanny resemblance to the stove portrayed in this photo, as does Hurley's earlier diagram.

"Potash and Pearlmutter,"—otherwise known as Orde-Lees and Green—who hauled a small sledge of cooking supplies and kitchen stores on the "second march," cooking hoosh at Patience Camp. Original nitrate.

"…our camp was a great sight today with masts & oars standing up in the snow & clothes beds boats & finscoes & blankets all out to dry any one would have thought it was our washing day. & it was far from that as we have not had our faces washed since we left the ship the only wash we have now is a rub with soft snow."

McNish diary
January 22, 1916

Original nitrate.

"Any one would have thought it was our washing day. & it was far from that…"

"*Carpenter finishes building topsides, forward, and after whalebacks on whaler [James Caird] and fits pump, made by Hurley, into her. All that now remains is to caulk her topsides. She could now, at a pinch carry 29 men. She can carry 6½ tons measurement of 3½ tons deadweight besides her gear.*"

WORSLEY DIARY
NOVEMBER 22, 1915

Original nitrate.

One of two small hoop tents at Patience Camp, draped with laundry. Original nitrate.

At Patience Camp,
the morning of
February 28, 1916
was spent building what
Reginald James termed,
"a noble edifice of ice
for a galley. It is circular
about 10' in diameter
with a wall 6' or 7' high
& it took a deal of ice."
Copy negative.

The James Caird *fitted with her "main mast" at Patience Camp. The two dogs pictured appear to be Nelson and Shakespeare. Original nitrate.*

The Dudley Docker
arrives at Elephant Island,
April 15, 1916. The
Stancomb-Wills and
James Caird had landed
first on "Providence
Beach," and the Docker,
piloted by Worsley, and
separated from the other
two the previous evening,
appeared after being feared
lost. All were saved!

The boats from
the Endurance
safely ashore on
Elephant Island

*Second view of hauling
the James Caird up
"Providence Beach,"
the Stancomb-Wills
and Dudley Docker in
the foreground. Greenstreet
and Blackborow, unable
to assist, are seated in the
background, on the left.
April 15, 1916.
Original nitrate.*

A *view of Elephant Island taken from the "spit" at the waterline. Original nitrate.*

The first hot drink
on Elephant Island,
April 15, 1916. Left
to right: Orde-Lees,
Wordie, Clark,
Rickenson, Greenstreet,
How, Shackleton,
Bakewell, Kerr, and
Wild. Original nitrate.

Another photo bearing
Hurley's name, but not
found among his original
nitrates. "A better day with
ocasional snow squalls,"
recorded Harry McNish on
April 20, 1916. "Started
to dismantle the Docker to
deck in the Caird."

Before Shackleton departed Elephant Island, the men had set to work chipping out space in a nearby glacier they imagined would provide shelter, a fact Shackleton later reported to newspapers.

One of two photos showing preparations to launch the Caird. Note the bags containing rocks for ballast and other supplies on the beach, April 24, 1916. Original nitrate.

Side view of preparations for launching the James Caird; Stancomb-Wills is in the foreground, April 24, 1916. Original nitrate.

The Stancomb-Wills *loading a water "beaker" on April 24, 1916 and about to make her way out to the James Caird; Shackleton is seated in the rear of the boat. Copy negative.*

Launching the James *Caird on Easter Monday, April 24, 1916. Ernest Shackleton's great voyage has begun.*

The start of the
most remarkable
ocean voyage
in history

The Stancomb-Wills
*prepares to deliver
Shackleton, seated in the
rear, to the* James Caird,
*April 24, 1916.
Original nitrate.*

*Once launched, the
Caird, top-heavy due to
Vincent's and McNish's
positions "topside," rolled
on her beam ends. Instead
of foundering, the two
men were tossed into the
sea and the Caird floated
free—straight toward
the rocks to the right,
April 24, 1916.
Original nitrate.*

Three cheers for the James Caird and her brave crew

Stores being transferred to the Stancomb-Wills *(just visible through the men) for transport to* the James Caird, *secured by a long painter, April 24, 1916. Original nitrate.*

The remaining Elephant Island party farewell Shackleton. This original nitrate was later altered by Frank Hurley to represent the rescue.

"Looking out of a rock cavern across West Bay, Elephant Island," reads the hand-lettered script in the Blue Album, manufactured by Raines & Company and presented to the King by Frank Wild on February 6, 1917. This photo, however, is not among Hurley's original nitrates.

On fine days the Elephant Island castaways were able to sneak around to the far side of the spit, exercising and hunting seals, and where they got a spectacular view of "Gnomon Island." Original nitrate.

The "hut" on Elephant Island before May 3, 1916. Hurley frequently used copy negatives of this image as a book illustration—after adding a hand-painted chimney not shown in this original nitrate.

"A pleasant, calm day, though dull"—early days on Elephant Island

"Pleasant calm day though dull. During the morning go walking with Wild. We visit a neighbouring cavern in the glacier which was adorned with a magnificence of icicles."

HURLEY DIARY
JULY 5, 1916

Original nitrate.

Gentoo penguins on the "spit" at Elephant Island. Copy negative.

Occasionally, the men were able to escape the Elephant Island "spit" and explore nearby parts of the island. Hurley, never one to sit still, climbed 400 feet (122 m) of rock on August 14 and captured this expansive view of the "hut" (barely visible on the "spit") and "Gnomon Island." Original nitrate.

One of two images not found among Hurley's original nitrates which show Gentoo penguins parading on the beach on Elephant Island.

Although this photo of penguins coming ashore on Elephant Island bears Hurley's name—as do all Endurance images—it is not among his original Kodak "plastic" negatives held in European archives.

"Skinning seals for
food on Elephant Island,"
wrote Hurley in his Green
Album, somewhere in
South America, as he
continued to add to, and
modify, the document.
Original nitrate.

The upturned-boat "hut" on Elephant Island just after its completion, but before the chimney was made and put in place by A. J. Kerr on May 3, 1916. Note the lack of snow surrounding the hut. Original nitrate.

Frank Hurley, holding a Vest Pocket Kodak—not the only camera he used to record life on Elephant Island—poses in front of the "Snuggery" midway through the ordeal. Note the elevation of snow surrounding the "sty." Original nitrate.

"Sunshiny day with gorgeous pink glow on the peaks at sunset. Took photo of group – the most motley and unkept assemblage that ever was projected on a plate," Hurley noted in his diary on May 10, 1916 on Elephant Island. Back row: Greenstreet, McIlroy, Marston, Wordie, James, Holness, Hudson, Stephenson, McLeod, Clark, Orde-Lees, Kerr, Macklin; middle row: Green, Wild, How, Cheetham, Hussey, Bakewell; in front: Rickenson. Missing from the photo are Hurley (who took it) and Blackborow, who was laid up with frostbitten toes. Original nitrate.

The Yelcho arrives at Elephant Island, August 30, 1916. A very different image from that seen in most accounts, portraying thick smoke from the beacon fire (far left) and what purports to be a ship on the horizon. Original nitrate.

Hurley's combination print, commonly found in the expedition literature, portraying the events, not as they actually were, on August 30, 1916.

Rescue at long last: their ordeal is finally at an end

Rescue at last,
August 30, 1916.
Original nitrate.

One of three photos of the Elephant Island rescue on August 30, 1916. However, this image is not among Hurley's original Kodak negatives.

Worsley, Pardo, and
Shackleton in the van at
Punta Arenas on
September 3, 1916.
Photograph by C. Veiga.

An image from the
Macleay Album, which
includes 18 silver gelatin
prints by Hurley. It
depicts the Yelcho's
departure from Punta
Arenas for Valparaiso on
September 15, 1916.

Pardo, Shackleton,
Wild, and others,
Punta Arenas,
September 3, 1916.
This is not thought to
be a Hurley photograph.

The rescued party
photographed in front
of the Royal Hotel,
Punta Arenas,
September 3, 1916.
Left to right: Hussey
(the only member
Shackleton allowed to
shave before reaching port),
Hurley, Kerr, James,
Wordie, Crean, Worsley,
Wild, Shackleton, Pardo,
Orde-Lees, Marston, (man
in tie: possibly John James
Gibbons Hardie), How,
Holness, Stephenson,
Bakewell, Green, McLeod,
Greenstreet, Cheetham.

Ice cliffs of Hamberg
Glacier, Moraine Fjord,
South Georgia, 1914.

Another view of
Rampart Berg, which
was visited by Hurley,
Wordie, and Worsley
on March 11, 1914.

While the origins of this photo are obscure, the figures here could possibly be Worsley and Greenstreet on their way up Duce Fell.

Glacier face. South Georgia, 1914.

The flensing plan at Grytviken, 1914. The building in the background is the Russebrake (the Russian Barracks).

A harpoon gun, loaded and ready to kill. During the 1914–15 season, over 5000 Leviathans of the deep, half of them Blue whales, were so dispatched.

Flensing plan, South Georgia, 1914. "During our last week the factory broke down and the supply of whale continued so that there were as many as 50 carcasses ... waiting to be delt with."

REGINALD JAMES
DIARY, 1914

A bull sea elephant with his harem at Hund Bay, November 17, 1914.

King penguins and their chicks photographed at Gold Harbor, South Georgia island, 1914. Copy negative.

Unafraid of humans:
the animal life of
South Georgia island

Grytviken, 1914.
During the 1914–15
season, South Georgia
whaling stations produced
370,507 barrels of oil.

Stromess. The manager's
villa, where Thoralf Sørlle
received Shackleton,
Worsley, and Crean on
May 20, 1916, is just to
the right of the photograph.

Cape pigeons feeding on whale parts cast off from a flensing plan in South Georgia.

King penguin rookery (right), Bay of Isles, South Georgia island.

Bull sea elephants fighting during the breeding season on South Georgia, photographed in 1914.

Geer Buttress and
Hooke Glacier, South
Georgia island. A small
copy of this print is found
in the Worsley collection of
photographs at the Scott

Polar Research Institute,
with the words, "Some of
the mountains we marched
across" scrawled on the
back of it.

The ice cliffs of Hamberg
Glacier, Moraine Fjord,
South Georgia, 1914.

SECTION FOUR
PIONEER OF POLAR PHOTOGRAPHY

PIONEER OF POLAR PHOTOGRAPHY

MICHAEL GRAY AND GAEL NEWTON

Some of Hurley's most dramatic examples of "extreme photography" came from a custom-built platform positioned on the port yardarm high above the deck of Endurance.

IN RECENT YEARS, a closer study of Frank Hurley's work than was done in his lifetime has revealed the extraordinary nature of his achievement, both as a photographer recording epic events and as a technical pioneer of his time.

The first publication of Hurley's images immediately after his return from the epic Imperial Trans-Antarctic Expedition in 1916, as the *Endurance* expedition was officially known, met with an enthusiastic reception. Hugh Lyall Watson, special correspondent of the Buenos Aires *Herald*, sent a piece to his newspaper after meeting Hurley for tea at Harrod's in Buenos Aires in 1916. It is clear from his descriptions of the photographs that Watson had a good understanding of the cultural and esthetic importance of Hurley's Antarctic imagery, going so far as to say that the pictures "changed forever the world view of the Antarctic Continent." Watson noted that "We do not see the glistening sheets of smooth ice so common in books of adventure. Instead there are hills and valleys and rough broken ground. Huge boulders and smaller pebbles are like nothing so much as rugged and rock-bound coast. But it is ice, made all the more wonderful by a covering of snow and rime which add to the majestic grandeur of the spectacle, which no imagination can conceive."

The 150 glass plate negatives Hurley brought back from the Antarctic, from an expedition whose epic story of survival was unique in the history of polar exploration, contained images of a violent and often terrifying world. Hitherto known only to a handful of people, it was dramatic and breathtakingly beautiful, dynamic, unpredictable, and unstable. The challenge for Hurley had lain as much in the danger and the uniqueness of the locations as in the opportunities for photography they had presented. Without a doubt, he sensed from the beginning that the Antarctic expedition was destined to be not only his greatest opportunity, but also his greatest challenge. Hurley's enduring achievement lay in the fact that he went far beyond his leader's initial brief, and his images remain an enduring record of human endeavor, endurance, and fortitude.

FRANK HURLEY AND THE *ENDURANCE* EXPEDITION

Frank Hurley had all the qualifications for the position of expedition photographer. His still photography and cinematographic work in the Antarctic had attracted considerable interest and praise worldwide, partly because of such films as *Home of the Blizzard*, premiered in Sydney in 1913 and later released in London. He also seemed to possess limitless reservoirs of energy, enthusiasm, and self-motivation.

Despite Hurley's experience of the Antarctic, a decisive factor in Shackleton's decision to take him as expedition photographer seems to have been financial. As Thomas Orde-Lees noted, "Short of funds to the tune of £25,000 to complete his expedition's finances, Sir Ernest was offered this sum by an influential syndicate on condition that he secured the services of the recently returned Mawson's Expedition cinematographer."

HURLEY, THE FIRST PRACTITIONER OF "EXTREME PHOTOGRAPHY"

From the outset of the expedition Hurley pushed both himself and the medium to their limits and there was virtually no subject or vista he did not attempt to capture and record, no matter how precarious or dangerous the vantage point. There are many passages in his diary, and in those of other members of the expedition, that illustrate the lengths to which he was prepared to go to obtain dramatic pictures in arduous and perilous conditions. An aspect of his character and makeup that set Hurley apart from other photographers working in harsh and hazardous conditions was his apparent disregard for personal safety. He was the first true practitioner of what we might call "extreme photography." It was not that he took the occasional chance; this primary drive was, it seemed, "hard-wired" into his persona. Time and again, his fellow expedition members commented on his activities, particularly on the outward journey when he was outside shooting whatever the weather.

Frank Worsley, captain of the *Endurance* and well used to seeing experienced, agile seamen working the rigging, frequently expressed concern for the Australian's safety. In this passage from his diary, Worsley's astonishment and surprise is clear: "Hurley the irrepressible who, perched like a chicken in the T'psail yardarm is taking a colour photo of the ship & ice… He is a marvel – with cheerful Australian profanity he perambulates alone aloft & everywhere, in the most dangerous & slippery places he can find, content & happy at all times but cursing so if he can get a good or novel picture. Stands bare [headed] & hair waving in the wind, where we are gloved & helmeted, he snaps his snap or winds his handle turning out curses of delight & pictures of Life by the fathom."

When he recounted the final moments of the *Endurance* in his book, *Endurance, an Epic of Polar Adventure*, Captain Worsley seemed to show more concern for Hurley than for the splintered remains of his once glorious ship. "The last work done by our cinematographer, Frank Hurley, before his valuable camera was thrown away, was to film the masts of the *Endurance* as these were slowly twisted from her by the overpowering ice flows. It took extreme care and wonderful judgment to enable him to film the masts as they came crashing down. So fine did he cut his distance that they swept within a few feet of where he was standing. His professional instincts were so strong, however, that he was too interested in having secured a unique picture to give a thought to the fact that he had come within an ace of disaster. But Hurley was a brave man."

There was also another side to this intrepid adventurer. When describing the location of one of his finest panoramic photographs taken from the heights overlooking Grytviken Whaling Station, South Georgia, Hurley showed himself to be appalled and deeply affected by the inherent contradiction that lay embedded within this image: "Apart from the transcending scenery, one is at once struck by the pungent effluviums which hang over the greasy waters. This is an emanation from the Grytviken Whaling Station, at the head of the Cove, & from innumerable derelict whale carcasses floating in the vicinity & lining the beach. Spinal columns, loose vertebrae, ribs & jaws being piled in heaps along the waterline, it is easy to count 100 huge skulls within a stone's throw. Over all crowns the pinnacle of Mt. Paget & the white mound of Sugartop, being majestic & mighty, yet even this magnificent scenery grows tainted through losing its splendour in the stench."

A week later his revulsion at the whaling trade was still just as strongly felt: "So polluted are the foreshores of King Edward Cove with offal & scrotts, that it is impossible to view this trade with other than loathing," he wrote. Once back home in Australia, Hurley did not forget his revulsion at the worst aspects of the whaling trade and he campaigned for the end of the slaughter.

A *cinecamera similar to this one was used by Frank Hurley to film the end of the* Endurance, *ignoring the dangers to obtain pictures unique in their dramatic immediacy.*

PHOTOGRAPHING THE DOOMED *ENDURANCE* AT NIGHT

The level of determination and commitment to his task shown by Frank Hurley becomes evident through close examination and study of several key images, in particular the series of the *Endurance* locked in pack-ice and photographed at night by magnesium flash (flare).

Two whole plate negatives of Endurance *encased in ice were taken by Hurley. This one was taken by flashlight during the night of August 27, 1915 and involved the use of 20 flashes.*

The *Endurance* was completely ice-bound and immobilized from February 24, 1915 until her final destruction and submersion on October 27. Between these two dates Hurley's options were as much determined by circumstance as by choice. He appears to have been given *carte blanche* to photograph at will, without the necessity of having to conserve or to save photographic materials for future use. It is probable that Shackleton thought the taking of photographs at night would occupy and help divert the attention of the crew and expedition members away from the seriousness of their situation.

Two whole plate negatives were taken of the *Endurance* encased in ice. Hurley described how he took one on Friday, August 27: "During the night take flashlight of the ship beset by pressure necessitating some 20 flashes, one behind each salient pressure hummock, no less than 10 flashes being required to satisfactorily illuminate the ship herself. Half blinded after the successive flashes, I lost my bearings amidst hummocks, bumping shins against projecting ice points & stumbling onto deep snow drifts &c. The negative when developed proved satisfactory & well repaid the cold endeavour."

It is extremely difficult to determine whether the two images are, in fact, positive or negative. Each image at first appears to be quite straightforward; a white or light sky set behind a darker complex mass of fine, delicate diagonal and angular lines floating above the white frost-encrusted hull, which in the first image is directed toward the photographer's left, while in the second, the *Endurance* is virtually side on to the camera. This tonal ambivalence can be seen at its most striking by comparing the two reproductions of the two images in their negative and positive states.

Hurley may have first thought of taking images at night on an earlier Antarctic trip; the inclusion of magnesium powder in his photographic supplies is an indication that he intended to experiment with night photography on this expedition. His immediate motivation for going to such lengths to capture the images may have been the difficulties inherent in photographing the rigging during the short period of daylight. Other factors could also have influenced his choice of night for his photography. For one thing, there was a lack of general contrast between the ship, the sky, and the thick, frost-encased masts and rigging. The flare would also have had a bearing, as would the near impossibility, in the darkroom, of being able to "hold back" or to "print in" such small, localized areas of tone.

WORK BEFORE PLAY

When the Elephant Island party was finally rescued on August 30, 1916, Hurley's first concern was the retrieval and preservation of his photographic negatives and undeveloped cinefilm stock. He noted in his diary: "…all gear which consisted of notes, photographic negatives, and a few sundries was carried to a suitable embarking rock, together with the invalid Blackborrow [sic]."

The reunited team arrived three days later at Punta Arenas, Chile, disembarking from the *Yelcho* on Sunday afternoon to a rapturous welcome from the local population. Hurley showed little inclination to rest or relax, however, and, despite allowing himself almost no time to recover from his Antarctic ordeal, his resilience and willpower seem to have survived intact.

On Monday afternoon, the day after his arrival, he made the acquaintance of a Mr Veiga, a photographer. "The leading photographer of the town placed his fine darkrooms at my disposal," Hurley recorded in his diary "and I spent most of the time in developing. All the plates which were exposed on the wreck nearly twelve months ago turned out excellently. The small Kodak film suffered through protracted keeping, but will be printable. Not all the individual frames are of equal density or condition. With the exception of three or four all are extremely thin with a density range which is only just printable… Mr Dixon, Chief Engineer, Chilean Navy, is having constructed a developing machine in order that I might run through my film (cine)."

Hurley turned down an invitation to attend the Governor's reception for the party, claiming that "photographic work exonerates me from these manifold engagements. This latter has been phenomenally successful, considering the vicissitudes through which it has passed and the fact that many of the films were exposed twelve months ago, and guarantee as per label ended about that time."

For three consecutive days Hurley worked assiduously in the dark, unable to rest until all films and plates had been processed. On Wednesday he spent the day developing cinema film. "The film exposed twelve months ago [September and onward, 1915] has lost nothing of its excellent quality."

Shortly after, Hurley arrived in London to deliver the *Endurance* footage and stills to Shackleton's film agent, Ernest Perris. Perris soon told Hurley what he already subconsciously knew: there was not enough wildlife and location footage to make a narrative feature for the public. Because of this, Hurley returned to South Georgia to shoot new footage, leaving London in mid-February 1917. The additional material enabled *In the Grip of the Polar Pack-ice* to be released several months later. Both the film itself, and a series of lectures illustrated with still photographs, were so successful that Shackleton was out of debt by July 1917.

The polar explorers at the turn of the twentieth century worked in a world where funding came from a wide range of private philanthropic, governmental, organizational, and commercial sources, and included advances for the exclusive rights to newspapers and films. For the public, the stirring stories of heroic struggles in the far-off ice lands of the Southern Oceans were both a model of courage and a respite from the horrors of the first war of the industrial age. It was this public consumption of the accounts of the expeditions that enabled the explorations to take place. The books, interviews, lectures, and films supplied by the leaders and members alike, were as vital to the expeditions as their prestigious reports to the scientific communities.

Although newspapers had only begun to include photomechanical reproductions in around 1904, both Captain Robert Scott on his British Antarctic Expedition (1910–13) and Dr. Douglas Mawson on the Australasian Antarctic Expedition (1911–14) knew that high-quality professional images were essential and appointed the first professional commercial photographers to their Antarctic expedition teams. Frank Hurley for Shackleton and Herbert Ponting for Captain Scott's South Pole expedition were instrumental in changing the way photography was used to record and document exploration.

This Prestwich No. 5 cinematographic 35 mm hand-cranked camera is similar to the one used by Hurley on the expedition.

This photograph, from an unpublished press advertisement made c. 1920 for Taylor Hobson and Cooke, shows "Series 3a lenses … for high speed subjects. Cinematography. Portraits," of the kind used by Hurley and Ponting.

ASSESSING THE WORK OF HURLEY AND PONTING

It is against Herbert Ponting's work as an Antarctic photographer that Hurley's achievements can be best assessed. Both Ponting and Hurley have just claims to being the first to bring the image of the Antarctic to a modern global public, and thus establishing popular notions of the south polar wilderness. They were both more than still photographers as they made films, gave lectures, and wrote books, and both were technically known for their great skill in camera operation and printing.

As professional, commercial photographers they were novelties in terms of traditional expedition management. They were in the Antarctic for business reasons, and in suspending other personal projects, were taking considerable financial risks.

As with all creative and technically skilled photographers, this mix of art and business presents challenges to the critical and historical assessment of their work. Both had wide-ranging careers, Ponting before, and Hurley for decades after their polar work. Hurley was prolific in his output and made himself highly visible by self-promotion throughout the many arenas of his career. His work spans the postcard trade and polar expeditions before World War One, war photography and cinematography in both World Wars, travel and expedition photography, films in the tropics, film production in the "talkies" of the 1930s and, finally, the extraordinary volume of Australian scenic publications, which kept him so busy from the 1940s to his death. However, being based in Australia, Hurley did slip out of sight in terms of the major canon of world photography.

Both Ponting and Hurley exhibited widely and disseminated spectacular large carbon prints of their work, which ensured the images a wider audience than if they had been reproduced only on newsprint, in books or on the ephemeral flickering cinema screen. Their carbon prints were made by the same firm in England and are similar in style, reflecting their joint heritage in the transitional years between the end of the "views" trade of the nineteenth century—original prints were marketed directly for sale but could not be mechanically reproduced— and the modern photojournalism of the 1930s, when such showcases for travel and expedition work as *Life* magazine (first published in 1936) were founded.

Surprisingly, Ponting's and Hurley's large carbon prints were not highly prized until the last decade of the twentieth century and interest in their work did not have any part in the activities of the wilderness society movements of the 1960s and 1970s.

Ponting, who came from a comfortable middle-class background, aimed his work at an educated and refined audience, and the better-illustrated papers. Hurley, a working-class boy from the colonies, was more a child of the modern newspaper and magazine era, the musical show, the cinema, and newsreels. The two men met in London in 1916, one effectively at the end of his creative life, the other only at the beginning. Each had a great respect for the other's achievements, both being self-taught and having chosen the life of roving outdoor travel photographer as a vocation. Together they had every right to feel they were masters of their medium.

Ponting was a model Edwardian esthete, and took pride in his refined sensibility. Nevertheless, he was tough enough physically to have coped well with a wide-ranging travel photography career before he joined Scott's expedition. Despite this experience, he was directed by Captain Scott to concentrate on his photography rather than take part in the general work of the expedition. Scott apparently feared that Ponting was not up to hard physical work and did not have the mental stamina for the dark winter months. Richard Ferguson, a present-day

Antarctic photographer and scholar, has noted "Despite having travelled widely in search of his photographs, Ponting was not included in any of the sledging parties that surveyed and explored the regions accessible from Cape Evans. As a compromise he had to make do with experiences limited to within the safe vicinity of the hut and a two-day outward journey accompanying the polar party. This greatly limited the realism of the images from the expedition because sledging on the ice shelf or the plateau occupied the largest proportion of the expedition's field work and Ponting had to stage many scenes for both still and moving images."

Hurley, on the other hand, was more or less given *carte blanche* by Shackleton not only to photograph anything he wished, but also to enlist the help of other expedition members in his endeavors. Perhaps because of this or because of his temperament, Hurley managed to create a visual record of the *Endurance* expedition to the Antarctic that was more personal and intimate than anything Ponting ever created.

The marked differences between the two men were reflected in their photography. Ponting sought a classical elegance and "tone" with his carefully composed images. His portrait studies, richly detailed, well-lit, carefully staged and usually close-up, are more powerful than Hurley's group shots, though the latter capture more of a sense of the close-packed, crumpled life in the huts and ships. Hurley's distinctive style of composition was characterized by open spaces with strong horizons, wide encompassing perspectives, deep focus, and sharp detail. It was then enlivened by dramatic lighting, cloud effects, a closer focus on animals and people, and bolder framing devices of the kind employed by romantic landscape photographers. Hurley had an affinity with wildlife, from Antarctic flora to the expedition's dogs, but Ponting had a far more poignant and subtle sense of figure placement in the landscape. In their Antarctic work, both photographers relied for some of their best effects on delicate black silhouetting of tiny figures against the immensity of the ice fields—a consequence not only of stylistic choice, but because properly exposed snow usually meant figures and faces were dark.

Taken by Frank Hurley, this photo, with its dramatic silhouetting of a small figure against the icy Antarctic wastes, shows stylistic similarities to the work of Herbert Ponting.

Both Ponting and Hurley had a marked technical and inventive side and both readily embraced new technologies of film and sound. It is hard now to understand the difficulties facing photographers working outdoors in the early twentieth century. Photographic equipment weighing 44 pounds (about 20 kg) was the norm for outdoor photography. Cameras in the 1900s were, in any case, large by modern standards and professionals preferred the larger formats—10 x 8 and 5 x 4—to the quarter plate cameras that were popular with amateurs. Furthermore, neither photographer had older experienced photographers to advise him on how to operate on any level, either technical or social, or on how to succeed in Antarctic photography. Hurley frequently noted in his diary the huge difficulties of operating a camera in the freezing conditions of the Antarctic. "My camera is a bug bear and using it is a nightmare," he wrote at one point. "Everytime I have to set the shutter I have to take a number of tiny screws from the front [with gloves off] and bend the mechanism into shape." During this process the screws would stick fast to his skin and have to be torn off.

Both men were part of a distinct shift toward beauteous landscape photography of subjects such as alpine scenes, or the wilder shores of the world, in the style pioneered in the late nineteenth century by photographers such as Adolphe Braun, Bisson Frères, and the Americans William Jackson and Eadweard Muybridge. In the face

Two views of the Kodak FPK No. 3a, the only camera Hurley had with him to photograph and document the expedition's long wait for rescue on Elephant Island.

of an ever-advancing urban industrial capitalist world, the new landscape offered idealists visions of the deep, empty spaces of a lost Garden of Eden.

Both also showed infinite patience in waiting for the right effect. Whereas Ponting would work only with what was in front of his camera, making repeated trips to the same vantage point looking toward Mount Fuji in Japan to secure one image through the grasses waving in the foreground, Hurley was perfectly happy to compose his image away from the subject, if necessary. He would have gladly climbed Mount Fuji and hung off a precipice to get his shot, but he would also have been ready to compose an image from grasses and clouds elsewhere, even in other countries, to get the effect he wanted. Hurley followed his father's advice to "find a way or make one" quite literally, particularly when it came to picture-making as opposed to picture-taking.

For Hurley, unlike Ponting, was, from the beginning, committed to delivering pictures to a broad audience. His montages and composites, begun in 1905, continued throughout his life, through dozens of Australian scenic books. In his images, clouds wander from place to place, people appear and disappear, overhanging branches are made to spawn a mirror pattern or frame different views, hills and mountains move from one image background to another, and a man rowing a dinghy appears on the same river in two different states. Sometimes these improvements occur in the same publication. Amusing and often disconcerting once revealed, these practices had no malicious or deceptive intent and are ultimately harmless, and even irrelevant in judging his work. Nevertheless it was these innovations that have proved to be a major factor in preventing "serious" recognition by the generations that followed Hurley. Throughout his life, he modified, retouched, and "repurposed" a significant number of his images as part of his quest for the "perfect" image.

HURLEY'S ESTHETIC

In one of his earliest articles, Hurley urged a broad attitude toward experimentation and control. Camera art was "not an exact representation of nature, and a picture is not a record of things in view," he wrote in an article on night photography in the *Australasian Photo-Review* in June 1911. "Regard your camera as an artist does his brush. Think that you hold a piece of apparatus worthy of the same possibilities as the artist… Your camera is but a piece of mechanical apparatus. You are its intellect."

However, he did not mean by this an endorsement of the idealized, subjective self-expression of his friends such as Norman Deck and Henri Mallard who practiced the soft-focus impressionistic studies of "fuzzy-wuzzy" Pictorialism. Temperamentally Hurley did not favor the close-up and the introspective in either his personal and social relations, or in his work. Life as a photographer meant being free to get outdoors and to be active and independent. He was obsessive about his work and resistant to excessive materialism. Ultimately his values of discipline and manly strength reflected those inculcated in the youth of his generation under the British Empire.

Hurley did not draw on the decorative or human interest motifs that feature in the work of older Pictorialists such as Harold Cazneaux (born 1878), whose stylish city scenes and landscapes dominated the Australian photography salons between 1910–30. Nor did he follow the younger avant-garde photographers born in the 1910s, such as Max Dupain and Olive Cotton, who adopted Modernism wholeheartedly and produced bold, low-angled architectural and industrial views, close-up portraiture, nudes, abstracted still lifes, and emotional sweeping landscapes. The social concerns of the Documentary movement, and the development of photojournalism were also not of interest.

Instead, Frank Hurley can be linked with an earlier generation of professional photographers who specialized in urban and landscape views demonstrating the progress of the country as it changed from being a British colony to becoming a nation in 1901. The basis of classic nineteenth-century "views" photography followed the traditions of topographical paintings, drawings and prints, which favored wide, deep, and often panoramic perspectives. Traditional topographical artists showed with pristine clarity the order being brought to an untamed land by settlement and construction.

Reaching adulthood at the turn of the century, Hurley was also heir to a very different style of photography that followed contemporary artistic trends, being acutely conscious of style, taste, and decorative effect. From studying the work of the art photographers who were prominent at the start of his career, and their photographs in magazines and journals such as *Amateur Photographer* and the annual *Photograms of the Year*, Hurley learned many techniques to make photographs more eye-catching and dramatic.

Hurley's work was phenomenally successful in the public domain even though in avant-garde circles he was seen as old-fashioned and tainted by his less-than-pure approach to picture making. With regard to overseas trends that developed in his lifetime, which many of his contemporaries followed, Hurley was probably unaware of modernists such as Edward Weston or of landscape photographers, such as Ansel Adams, whose modernist styles dramatized monumental views.

At its most altruistic, Hurley's esthetic ideal was one in which nature was to be improved upon and made into art. His goal was never to be merely representational, but to produce a powerful image based on his subject. His idealism was that of the epic film editor; cinematography was born in his lifetime and Hurley was one of Australia's early professional cameramen. He was never a documentary photographer or cinematographer in the current sense. His reportage work was done in a period of transition before the 1930s concept of unmanipulated truthful framing and shooting for a "decisive moment" became one of the ideologies of Documentary photography and photojournalism.

Travel photography had been well-established in the nineteenth century and there was no shortage of photographers who were intrepid in their quest for the first pictorial booty to be brought back to Europe. Hurley was not merely a visual scout, but was very much the creator of his images. Photography had passed from being a neutral record, and the tasteful public face of history, to being the generator of dynamic images for a highly competitive, international media. Frank Hurley worked for the public, not for his peers. He brought the most rigorous standards to taking perfectly exposed, deep-focus negatives, but the classic unities of time and space were secondary if they obstructed the narrative. He would have been proud to be recognized for not only taking but also making attractive pictures to entertain, inform, and involve his audience. In this, as well as in his exceptional skill and—in his own terms—his powerful will, he "found a way and made it," and can justly be regarded as one of the twentieth century's greatest pioneers of photography.

Hurley's pride in Australia's progress from colony to nation is implicit in this fine photo of Sydney Harbour Bridge, taken in the 1940s.

FRANK HURLEY'S CAMERAS, EQUIPMENT, AND MATERIALS

THE START OF THE twentieth century was a time of great innovation and change for photography. The introduction of roll film cameras using cellulose-nitrate base led eventually to the replacement of glass by plastic as the primary emulsion support. However, the process took far longer than originally anticipated; it would be another fifty years before the introduction of Estar-based plastics permitted close, accurate registration for color and duotone origination for pre-press print production and the graphic arts. As late as the mid-1960s, glass plate was still in common use in certain sectors of the photographic profession.

The introduction of the small portable roll film camera by George Eastman (later Eastman-Kodak) in 1897 was at first aimed exclusively at the amateur market, with the Folding Pocket Kodak retailing at just eight dollars. They were considered by professionals to be little more than toys. Even the next generation of Kodaks, the VPK No. 3, introduced in 1900, and the later FPK No 3A, following on from the introduction of the first Brownies, were not nearly as robust and durable as the equivalent European cameras—such as a Göertz Anschütz—of the same format.

Thus, when Frank Hurley was assembling his equipment for the *Endurance* expedition, the range of benefits available from the new films and cameras was not sufficient to persuade him to discard the old in favor of the new. It was not just that professional photographers were more accustomed to handling and working with glass negatives: film was more difficult to spot and retouch than glass; it was more easily damaged; and the longevity and stability of early film was open to question. For the professional, cost was never the first consideration. Cameras were—and still are—considered to be tools of the trade: quality, reliability, and durability are the foremost criteria in photographers' minds.

Endurance Expedition Equipment

There is no absolutely definitive list of the apparatus and equipment Hurley actually assembled to take with him on the expedition, because the two primary documentary sources—an article published in the *Australasian Photo-Review* in August, 1922, and an inventory made by Hurley at Ocean Camp—vary to some degree. We know less about his basic black and white work then we do about his Paget Colour or cinephotography. The fact that there are discrepancies and contradictions between the various accounts may indicate that he took a greater variety of instruments on the voyage, and possibly that there were a number that were never used.

Cameras

Hurley's equipment included three Folmer & Schweig Graflex cameras (the company had been taken over by Eastman Kodak in 1905, to become the Folmer & Schweig division of Eastman-Kodak). All three were fitted with Cooke lenses made by Taylor Hobson and Cooke of Leicester, England.

It is not clear whether all three Graflex cameras were the same model or variants. Nevertheless, it is fairly safe to assume that at least one of the three would have been Folmer & Schweig's Naturalist Graflex of 1907, which, according to Brian Coe, former curator of the Kodak Museum in London, had a "considerable focusing extension, which gave it the capacity to accommodate long-focus lenses." The instrument was quite large, bulky, and unwieldy, requiring a strong stable tripod to be used at all times. The viewing hood incorporated a mirror, so that the camera could be used at eye-level and the eyepiece could be turned into a vertical position. There are at least two references indicating that a number of photomicrographs were taken of mosses, lichens, and other small organisms, and this would have required a long bellows extension.

Two other models that came out around the same time were the 3a Graflex (1907) and the 1a Graflex

---

Inventory of all known cameras

The following inventory of Hurley's equipment on the *Endurance* expedition is based on an article in the *Australasian Photo-Review* in August, 1922 (APR) and the inventory made by Hurley at Ocean Camp (OCI).

Camera Equipment (Still)

3 Folmer & Schweig Graflex, single lens reflex camera, introduced 1904, 120 x 178 mm (APR); 1 Vest Pocket Kodak, VPK No. 3, folding pocket self-erecting bellows camera, introduced 1900, 83 x 108 mm (APR); 1 Folding Pocket Kodak, FPK No. 3a, folding pocket self-erecting bellows camera, introduced 1900, 83 x 140 mm (3) (APR); 1 Göertz Anshütz, folding (collapsing strut) box camera, introduced 1905, 108 x 170 mm (half plate) (OCI); unidentified whole plate, square bellows, mahogany/brass, rising/cross front, 170 x 215 mm (whole plate), (two, same format, unidentified maker) (APR); 1 Panoramic Camera Kodak No. 4 Panoram (1899), 83 x 305 mm (OCI).

Camera Equipment (Movie)

Prestwich No. 5 Cinecamera, introduced 1901; Newman and Sinclair Cinecamera (APR); microcinema outfit, unidentified (APR).

Lenses

12-inch f3.5 (APR); Mooy/Hurley, Ross Telecentric, 17-inch f5.4 (APR); Cooke Optical Co. Cine, unidentified, various.

(1910). Hurley might have preferred the original Press Graflex for general hand-work on and around the *Endurance* during periods of bright sunlight because of its focal plane shutter and maximum speed of 1200th of a second. It came with a combination back capable of taking both roll film and 5 x 7 inch glass plate holders.

The Ocean Camp Inventory also includes a Göertz Anshütz camera, a sturdy piece of apparatus which would have been the preferred choice of a professional over the smaller, lighter Kodak camera in normal circumstances. Its wooden construction and few metal parts would have been much easier to operate and would have offered more protection to the film against extremes of temperature than metal-bodied cameras. With temperatures often many degrees below freezing, the photographer's skin could inadvertently become stuck to any bare metal parts of the camera. The German camera was whole-plate, which makes it the most likely camera to have been used by Hurley earlier on board the *Endurance*, and, later, at Ocean and Patience camps. It was only after the loss of the *Endurance* that Hurley had no alternative other than to retain the FPK 3A and three rolls of film.

The "cinematographic camera" was the Prestwich No. 5, one of the earliest British movie cameras based on the original design by William Friese-Greene. It incorporated an improved and redesigned film transport mechanism found in the Prestwich No. 1. The original sprocket mechanism was designed and built by Friese-Greene, but little else is known of the history or background of this early 35 mm cinecamera.

Also included was "a microcinema outfit," perhaps the most intriguing item of all. Unless Hurley had acquired a device of unknown origin or manufacture, the only micro-cinecameras known to be available and in small-scale production at this time were the Tourist Multiple Camera, which first appeared on the market in 1913, and Sinclair's Centrum Film Camera, which according to Brian Coe was not available early in 1915, and so would seem to have been too late to have been taken on the expedition. The Tourist Multiple Camera may possibly have been supplied through Kodak, Australia, but the *Australasian Photo-Review* article does not shed light on this.

However, there are circumstantial factors that support the notion that Hurley, or perhaps Shackleton, may have been supplied with one of Sinclair's proto-types for the purposes of evaluation on the expedition.

Glass plate negatives and film used:

"Austral" (Eastman-Kodak) Standard plates (backed) 120 x 178 mm (5 x 7 inches) (APR); "Austral" Lantern (Eastman-Kodak) 120 x 178 mm (5 x 7 inches) (APR); Imperial SR (special rapid) (Imperial Dry Plate Company, Cricklewood) 170 x 215 mm (whole plate 8½ x 6¼ inches) (OCI); Imperial (ordinary) (Imperial) 170 x 215 mm (whole plate 8½ x 6¼ inches) (OCI); Strippable ordinary (Imperial) 170 x 215 mm (whole plate 8½ x 6¼ inches) (OCI); Imperial (ordinary) (Imperial) 170 x 108 mm (half plate 4¼ x 6¼ inches) (OCI); Autochrome plates color transparency (Autochrome) 170 x 108 mm (half plate 4¼ x 6¼ inches) (OCI).

Cellulose-nitrate film used:

Cellulose-nitrate stock, black and white (Eastman-Kodak) 127 mm and 118 mm format (OCI); Paget Colour transparency film plus Paget screens, 127 mm format (OCI).

The OCI lists only the Imperial Dry Plate Company's glass photographic plate negative stocks. In contradiction the APR article declares: "Hurley to be taking the best photographic equipment ... the whole of it supplied by Kodak."

Not one of the single 5 x 7 inch glass plate negatives survives, nor one specimen of a nitro-cellulose negative of the same format. A small number of half plate original negatives have survived and possibly a number of other images, but only in the form of copy negatives where the verification of film type and format is now no longer possible.

The inventory lists one-and-a-half gross (216) whole plate "strippable ordinary" glass negatives. The fact that Hurley had such a large quantity of strippable negatives is extremely interesting in light of suggestions that Hurley made copies of some of the negatives.

There were (and still are) two principal ways in which a photograph can be copied. The most common method is to make an enlarged print from the negative, preferably on matte paper, using a soft-working metol developer; shadow detail would be protected as much as possible and the whole photograph would be printed somewhat gray and light. All subsequent retouching and painting-in is matted by overpainting with gum Arabic or sanderac varnish, and the finished print is rephotographed.

The second method, technically more difficult and costly, produces a far better result. It entails using the specialized "stripping film" mentioned above. This process involves contact printing the original negative on to a second plate, resulting in a same-size positive image on glass. The process is then repeated once more to turn the interpositive image back to one that is negative. This minimizes the loss of highlight or shadow details to such a degree that only close examination by an expert can reveal any difference between the two versions. Apart from a slight suggestion of flare running along all four outer edges of the glass, there would be virtually no way to distinguish between the original and the copy.

It is possible that Hurley, without bothering to inform either Shackleton or any of his colleagues, brought back additional copies or even original negative images interleaved between the pages of a book. This could possibly account for some of the apparent discrepancies that still exist regarding the exact number of negatives that were brought back from the expedition.

Hurley was extremely skilled, inventive, and versatile, a complete photographer in every respect, both in theory and practice, behind the camera and in the darkroom. If we must accept that we will never be able to prove with any real certainty which of his negatives are original and which are second-generation surrogates, this should be seen as a lasting tribute to the level of his skill and technical excellence.

Frank Hurley: A Chronology

1885: James Francis Hurley born in Glebe, Sydney, New South Wales on October 15.

1898: Quits school and jumps a freight train, ending up in the mining town of Lithgow; works as assistant fitter in ironworks.

c. **1900:** Returns to Sydney and undertakes various jobs, doing technical training courses at night.

c. **1902–3:** Interest in photography begins. Purchases first camera, Kodak box camera.

c. **1904:** Employed by the Telegraph Department and learns electrical instrument work. First photography commission.

1905: First published photograph, a seascape, appears in June 21 issue of *Australasian Photo-Review*.

c. **1907–8:** Goes into partnership with Henry Cave producing postcards.

1910: Company's Power & Speed postcard series are best-sellers; Hurley a founder member of the Ashfield Camera Club. Exhibition of photographs at the Kodak showroom, Sydney. May have begun learning to use a movie (cinematograph) camera this year.

1911: On the committee of the New South Wales Photographic Society's interstate Salon; by now is regularly publishing articles on photography. The postcard business in recession and as his partner, Henry Cave retires from the business, Hurley is forced to cut down his business. Meets Dr. Douglas Mawson and is taken on as photographer for the first Australian scientific expedition to the Antarctic. Team leaves Hobart for the Antarctic on board the *Aurora* on December 2.

1913: Returns from the Antarctic. Film *Home of the Blizzard* premieres in Sydney. Returns to the Antarctic, mid-November, on *Aurora*, sent to pick up Mawson, and spends 10 days at Adélie Land photographing flora and fauna.

1914: Joins cinematographer Francis Birtles on four-month overland motoring tour of the far north of Australia, with a commission from Australasian Films Ltd. While on tour, is recruited by Sir Ernest Shackleton as photographer on Imperial Trans-Antarctic Expedition. Joins up with Shackleton and other expedition members in Buenos Aires in October, sailing for South Georgia on the *Endurance* on October 26. After a month in South Georgia, *Endurance* leaves for the Weddell Sea on December 5.

1915: *Endurance* locked in pack-ice, January 19. Hurley photographs the end of the *Endurance*, November, having salvaged film and equipment from the wreck.

1916: April 9, expedition members take to the boats and after six days and nights reach Elephant Island. Shackleton leaves in *James Caird* to get help, taking with him some of Hurley's photographs, one

of which appears in *Daily Mirror* in July. *Yelcho* arrives at Elephant Island to rescue the expedition members, August 30. Hurley arrives in London, November.

1917: Spends a month in South Georgia, photographing wildlife. Film *In the Grip of the Polar Pack-ice* released and is a financial success. As official photographer for the Australian Army, with the rank of captain, arrives in Flanders in August. Sent on to Palestine, December.

1918: Marries Antoinette Theirault-Leighton in Cairo in April. Returns to England to organize photographic section of exhibition devoted to Australian Infantry Force in London. Leaves army, July, and returns to Cairo, joins Antoinette and leaves for Australia, arriving on November 11.

1919: Twin daughters, Antoinette and Adelie, born. Spends year consolidating position as photographer and lecturer. Invested with Polar Medal and clasp.

1920: Joins Ross and Keith Smith for their last leg, northern Queensland-Sydney, of their 30-day flight from the UK. Film taken on the flight forms the basis of the film *The Ross Smith Flight*. Accepts commission from Anglican Board of Missions to make a film of their work in New Guinea.

1921: Daughter, Yvonne, born. Film *The Heart of New Guinea* released. Exhibition of Papua New Guinea photographs at Kodak Gallery, Sydney.

1922–23: Part-travelogue, part-ethnographic film *Pearls and Savages* released. Tours Australia, photographing the landscape, with fellow-photographer Harry Phillips. Organizes a second expedition to Papua New Guinea, for which he forms company called World Picture Exploration with the aim of making travel films. After the expedition, releases an up-dated version of *Pearls and Savages* and a new film, *With the Headhunters of Unknown Papua*. Fourth child, Frank Jr., born in 1923.

1924: Tours America, giving a series of lectures and film screenings. Two books by Hurley, *Pearls and Savages* and *Argonauts of the South*, published by New York publisher G. P. Putnam's Sons. Tours England with film *Pearls and Savages*, selling the rights to the film to a German company.

1925–26: Sets up as an independent film studio. Two feature films, *The Jungle Woman* and *Hound of the Deep*, released in 1926. Begins broadcasting on radio.

1927–28: Sells a large number of his New Guinea negatives to the Australian Museum in Sydney. Acts as picture editor for the *Sun* newspaper, Sydney. Organizes to beat flying record between Sydney and London, but crashes in Athens. Spends some time in England working as a cameraman in a film studio.

1929–30: Takes part in two British, Australian, and New Zealand Research Expeditions (BANZARE) to the Antarctic organized by

Sir Douglas Mawson, and obtains much useful film footage on both. Film *Southward Ho!* released in 1930.

1931: Accepts salaried position with Cinesound, a subsidiary of Greater Union Theatres, and begins working on documentary films.

1933: On the team that makes the second "talkie" to be made in Australia, *The Squatter's Daughter*.

1936: Is placed in charge of a new industrial film department, which takes on commissioned films for corporations and industrial organizations.

1938: Work features prominently in publications issued to mark the 150th anniversary of European settlement in Australia, for which he also makes the Cinesound documentary *A Nation is Born*.

1939: Works as an outdoor cameraman on Charles Chauvel's epic film, *Forty Thousand Horsemen*. After Australia declares war in October, Hurley is appointed to the national broadcast radio, ABC, as a reporter.

1940: With an acting major's rank, is appointed to oversee the Official Cinematographic and Photographic Unit in the Middle East and, by the end of the year, is following British and Imperial forces in North Africa.

1941: Moves with the photographic unit to Syria. Awarded an OBE for his war photographic work.

1946–47: Returns to Australia in September 1946. Decides not to return to the post-war travelogue-documentary or feature film business, and turns to book publishing. Also begins broadcasting on radio again.

1948: Publishes *Shackleton's Argonauts* and *Sydney: A Camera Study*.

1949: Publishes *The Holy City: A Camera Study of Jerusalem and Its Surroundings*.

1950s: Journeys widely across Australia photographing the country for the many books and (from 1953) the scenic postcards and calendars that will provide the popular national and international image of Australia for nearly two decades. A best-seller of the period is *Australia, A Camera Study*, published in 1955.

1962: January 16, Frank Hurley dies at his home in Sydney.

1966: A biography of Frank Hurley, *Once More on my Adventure*, written jointly by his daughter Antoinette and Frank Legg, is published.

Acknowledgments and Bibliography

ACKNOWLEDGMENTS

The authors wish to thank the Alexander Turnbull Library/Te Puna Mātauranga o Aotearoa, Wellington, New Zealand; the Buenos Aires *Herald* newspaper, Argentina; Dartmouth College Library, Hanover, USA; the Mitchell Library, State Library of New South Wales, Sydney, Australia; and the Scott Polar Research Institute, University of Cambridge, England, for permission to use material quoted in the text. The quotation on page 12 is included with the permission of the owners, obtained via Shane Murphy.

Thanks are also extended to: The Royal Geographical Society, London; The Royal Photographic Society, Bath; The National Museum of Photography Film and Television; The Science Museum, Bradford; State Library of New South Wales; The National Library of Australia, Canberra; University of Bath Library, Bath; Central Reference Library, Bath; British Library, London; and Cooke Optical Company, New Jersey; John Adderley; Douglas Arnold; Alan Davies; David Gray; Barbara Gray; Michael Harvey; Stephen Herbert; Richard Kossow; David and Cathy Liliburn; Barbara Lowry; Hazel Piper; Brett Rogers; Joe McNeilage; Pamela Roberts; Philippa Smith; Lucy Martin; William Mills, Keeper and Librarian at the Scott Polar Research Institute; Joanna Wright; and Dr Andrew Tatham, Keeper of Collections at the Royal Geographical Society. In particular to Gordon Trewinnard, for permission to photograph his Prestwich No. 5.

RESOURCES and READING LIST
Primary Sources

Much invaluable material about the Imperial Trans-Antarctic Expedition is contained in unpublished diaries, memoirs and other writings, particularly by those who sailed on board the *Endurance*, which are held in libraries and research centres in several countries. Those that were consulted by the three authors of *South with Endurance* are listed below. Abbreviations in the list are: ATL, Alexander Turnbull Library/ Te Puna Mātauranga o Aotearoa; DCL, Dartmouth College Library; ML, Mitchell Library, State Library of New South Wales; SPRI, Scott Polar Research Institute.

Australian Film Institute, bibliography: www.cinemedia.net/AFI/biblioz/hurl-bib.html
Bakewell, Mrs., letter dated March 5, 1972, see page 68
Bakewell, William, answers to written questions from James Fisher (SPRI MS1456/78)
Blackborow, John, handwritten monograph by Perce Blackborow, "Lecture given to Belt Street School, Pill, Newport and the Y.M.C.A." accompanied by a transcribed typewritten copy
British Film Institute's re-release of *South* in 1998
Deane, Robert, "Australian military photography, WWI-II Frank Hurley to George Silk" (paper presented at Revealing the Holy Land seminar, National Gallery of Australia, Canberra, April 30, 2000 and now in the gallery's MS Research Library)
Greenstreet, Lionel, conversation with James Fisher (SPRI MS1456/70)
How, Walter, conversation with James Fisher (SPRI, MS 1456/70)

Hurley, James Francis (Frank), answers to written questions from James Fisher (SPRI MS 1456/78)
Green Album (photograph album) (SPRI, P66/19)
original diaries and edited typescript (ML MSS 389/2, 389/3–4, ZML MSS389/5)
James, R. W. (Reginald), answers to written questions from James Fisher (SPRI MS 1456/78)
journals (SPRI, MS370/1–5)
Mawson, Douglas, archive, Mawson Antarctic Collection, Waite Campus, University of Adelaide
McNish, Harry, diary (ATL, MS1389)
Mooy, Toni, personal correspondence to Shane Murphy, see page 97
Murphy, Shane, *Shackleton's Photographer: Frank Hurley's Diaries 1914–1917* (CD-Rom in Acrobat READER see www.frankhurley.com)
National Film and Sound Archive's 1933 film *Endurance*, Worsley's narrative of the story of the *Endurance* Expedition to a young boy
Orde-Lees, Thomas, diary (ATL, MS papers 0405v)
diary (DCL, MS 185)
diary (SPRI, MS 967/3/1–2)
ScreenSound Australia (National Film and Sound Archive) Canberra, video/film tapes of interviews by Martha Ansara: www.screensound.gov.au.
Wild, Frank, Memoirs (ML MS 2198), with the permission of Mrs. Anne Fright. The original diary is held in the Mitchell Library, State Library of New South Wales
Worsley, Frank, diaries (SPRI, MSS 297, 637, 732)

Secondary Sources

Ansara, Martha, "A Few Words about Frank Hurley," Metro, 115, 1998
Alexander, Caroline, *The Endurance: Shackleton's Legendary Antarctic Expedition*, Bloomsbury, London, 1998 and Alfred Knopf, New York, 1999
Armstrong, Jennifer, *Shipwreck at the Bottom of the World*, Crown Publishers, New York, 1998
Arnold, H. J. P., *Photographer to the World: The Biography of Herbert Ponting*, Fairleigh Dickenson University Press, Rutherford, 1971
Australasian Photo-Review, especially March 22, 1909 and March 23, 1914
Bickel, Lennard, *In Search of Frank Hurley*, Macmillan, Sydney, 1980
Boddington, Jennie, *Antarctic Photographs 1910–1916, Herbert Ponting and Frank Hurley*, St Martin's Press, New York, 1979
Brune, Peter and McDonald, Neil, *200 Shots: Damien Parer and George Silk and the Australians at War in New Guinea*, Allen & Unwin, Sydney, 1998
Cato, Jack, *The Story of the Camera in Australia*, Georgian House, Melbourne, 1955, reprinted Institute of Australian Photographers/ Methuen, 1977
Cockram, Roy, *The Antarctic Chef: the Story of Charles Green*, Southampton, 1999
Coe, Brian, *Cameras, from Daguerreotypes to Instant Pictures*, Crown Publishing Inc., New York, 1978
Daily Chronicle newspaper, London, May–August, 1914, May–August, 1916, and September–December 1916
Dunnett, Harding McGregor, *Shackleton's Boat – The Story of the James Caird*, Neville & Harding Ltd, Kent, 1996

Ferguson, Richard G., *The Hurley-Mawson View of Antarctica: A Contemporary View*, manuscript 1997, Melbourne, author's copy
Fisher, James and Margery, *Shackleton*, London, 1957
Heacox, Kim, *Shackleton: The Antarctic Challenged*, The National Geographic Society, Washington, 1999
Herald newspaper, Buenos Aires, Argentina, especially 1914–1916
Hurley, Frank, *Argonauts of the South*, G. P. Putnam's Sons, New York, 1925
Hurley, Frank, *Pearls and Savages*, G. P. Putnam's Sons, New York, 1924
Hurley, Frank, *Shackleton's Argonauts*, Angus & Robertson, Sydney, 1948
Jolly, Martyn, "Australian First World War Photography: Frank Hurley and Charles Bean," *History of Photography*, vol. 23, no. 2, Summer 1999
Kay, Philip, *The Far-Famed Blue Mountains of Harry Phillips*, Megalong Books, Second Back Row Press, Leura, New South Wales, 1985
Mawson, Sir Douglas, *The Home of the Blizzard; Being the Account of the Australasian Antarctic Expedition*, Lippincott, Philadelphia, 1915
Millar, David P., *From Snowdrift to Shellfire: Capt. James Francis (Frank) Hurley 1885–1962*, David Ell Press, Sydney, 1984
Mooy (née Hurley), Toni, in collaboration with Legg, Frank, *Once More on My Adventure*, Ure Smith, Sydney, 1966
Newton, Gael, *Going to Extremes: George Silk Photojournalist* (exhibition brochure), National Gallery of Australia, Canberra, 2000
Newton, Gael, *Silver and Grey: Australian Photography 1900–1950*, Angus and Robertson, Sydney, 1980
Newton, Gael, *Shades of Light: Photography and Australia 1839–1988*, National Gallery of Australia, Collins Australia, Sydney, 1988
O'Keefe, Daniel, *Hurley at War: The Photography and Diaries of Frank Hurley in Two World Wars*, Fairfax Library, Sydney, 1986
Ponting, Herbert G., *The Great White South*, Duckworth, London 1921
Shackleton, Sir Ernest, *South: a Memoir of the Endurance Voyage*, Macmillan, New York, 1920
Smith, Michael, *An Unsung Hero: Tom Crean – Antarctic Survivor*, The Collin Press, Cork, 2000
Specht, James and Fields, John, *Frank Hurley in Papua: Photographs of the 1920–23 Expeditions*, Robert Brown and Australian Museum Trust, Sydney, 1984
Spufford, Francis, *I May Be Some Time*, Faber & Faber, London, 1996
Sydney Morning Herald newspaper, Australia, especially March 6, 1914
The Lone Hand (Australian magazine), especially January 2, 1911 and November 2, 1914
Thomas, Julian, "The Best Country in the World," *Showman: The Photography of Frank Hurley*, National Library of Australia, Canberra, 1990
Thompson, John, *Hurley's Australia, Myth, Dream, Reality*, National Library of Australia, Canberra, 1999
Thompson, John, *Shackleton's Captain: A Biography of Frank Worsley*, Mosaic Press, New York, 1999
Worsley, Frank, *Endurance: An Epic of Polar Adventure*, Jonathan Cape, London and Harrison Smith, New York, 1931
Worsley, Frank, *Shackleton's Boat Journey*, W. W. Norton & Co, New York, 1977

Photography Credits

The majority of the photographs in this book are from the Royal Geographical Society, Scott Polar Research Institute, and the State Library of New South Wales.

Photographs from the Royal Geographical photographic archive © Royal Geographical Society appear on pages: 2, 5, 7, 8–9, 9 (inset), 10, 13, 14 (bottom), 15, 16 (top), 17 (top and bottom), 18, 19 (top), 20, 21, 22, 23, 24, 27 (top and bottom), 28, 29, 32–33, 61, 64–65, 65 (inset), 66, 67 (top), 68 (right), 69, 70–71, 72, 73, 74, 75 (both), 76, 77 (top), 78 (both), 79, 80, 81 (left), 84, 85 (both), 86, 88 (both), 89, 92, 93 (top), 96, 100, 102, 103, 104, 108, 109 (top), 114, 115, 116 (both), 118 (both), 119, 120, 121, 122, 123, 124, 125, 126, 128, 131, 132, 133, 134, 135, 136, 138 (bottom), 139, 140, 141, 142, 143 (top left and bottom), 144, 145 (far left, top left), 148, 149, 154, 155, 156, 157 (right), 158, 159, 160, 161, 162, 163, 164, 165, 166 (right), 167, 168, 169, 170, 172, 173, 174–175, 176, 177, 178, 179, 180, 181, 182, 183, 184, 185, 186, 187, 188, 189, 190, 191, 192, 193, 194, 195, 196, 197, 198, 199, 200, 201, 202, 203, 204, 205, 206, 207, 208, 209, 210, 211, 212, 213, 214, 215 (bottom), 216, 218, 219, 221, 222, 223, 226, 227 (bottom), 228, 229, 230–231, 232, 234 and 237

Photographs from the Scott Polar Research Institute photographic archive © Scott Polar Research Institute appear on pages: 12, 14 (top), 16 (bottom), 19 (bottom), 31, 62–63, 63 (bottom), 67 (bottom), 68 (left), 77 (bottom), 81 (right), 93 (bottom), 97 (all), 98 (all), 99, 101 (both), 105, 109 (bottom), 112–113, 117 (both), 127, 129 (all), 130, 137, 138 (top), 143 (top right), 145 (top right, bottom left, bottom right), 152 (both), 153 (both), 157 (left), 166 (left), 171, 215 (top and middle), 217, 220 (both), 224, 225 and 227 (top)

Photographs from the State Library of New South Wales photographic archive © State Library of New South Wales appear on pages: 3, 30, 34, 39, 42, 43, 46, 82, 83, 87, 90, 91, 94, 95, 106, 107, 110, 111, 146, 147, 150 and 151

In addition, the following photos appear in this book.

Page 11 Reproduced map of the *Endurance* expedition voyage
Courtesy of the Royal Geographical Society

Page 26 Pages from Frank Hurley's Antarctic diary
Courtesy of the Image Library, State Library of New South Wales.

Page 35 *"Sydney Harbour Bridge from Circular Quay,"* c. 1940
Frank Hurley 1885–1962
Frank Hurley Collection
National Library of Australia, Canberra
© National Library of Australia

Page 36 *"Power and Speed,"* c. 1910
Frank Hurley 1885–1962
Plate from *The Lone Hand*, January 2, 1911

Page 37 *"Sydney Post Office by Night, from Barrack Street,"* c. 1908
Frank Hurley 1885–1962
Cave and Hurley postcard
Private Collection

Page 38 *"Breaking Wave, Sydney,"* c. 1905–10
Frank Hurley 1885–1962
National Gallery of Australia, Canberra, Kodak
(Australasia) Pty Ltd Fund, 1992

Page 40 *"Royal Penguins on Nugget's Beach, Macquarie Island,"* 1911
Frank Hurley 1885–1962
National Gallery of Australia, Canberra, Kodak
(Australasia) Pty Ltd Fund, 1992

Page 41 *"Out in the Blizzard, Winter Quarters, Main Base, Cape Denison, Adelie Land,"* 1912
Frank Hurley 1885–1962
National Gallery of Australia, Canberra, Kodak
(Australasia) Pty Ltd Fund, 1992

Page 45 *"Playmates—Native Child and Puppy, Northern Queensland,"* 1914
Frank Hurley 1885–1962
National Gallery of Australia, Canberra, Kodak
(Australasia) Pty Ltd Fund, 1992

Page 47 *"An Australian Light Horseman Picking Anemones, Belah, Palestine,"* 1917
Frank Hurley 1885–1962
Australian War Memorial, Canberra
© Australian War Memorial

Page 50 *"The Morning after the First Battle at Passchendaele, Flanders,"* October 9, 1917
Frank Hurley 1885–1962
Frank Hurley Collection
National Library of Australia, Canberra
© National Library of Australia

Page 51 Antoinette Thierault-Leighton with Captain Frank Hurley at the time of their marriage, Cairo, April 1918
Unknown photographer
Copy photograph courtesy of the National Library of Australia, from *Once More on my Adventure*, Frank Legg in collaboration with Toni Mooy, 1966.
See also page 33

Page 52 *"The Author Recording a Concert at Aramia,"* Papua New Guinea, 1921
Frank Hurley 1885–1962
Frank Hurley Collection
National Library of Australia, Canberra
© National Library of Australia

Page 55 *"Trusty Friends in Adventure."* BANZARE Expedition 1929–1930
Frank Hurley 1885–1962
Frank Hurley Collection
National Library of Australia, Canberra
© National Library of Australia

Page 57 Damien Parer, Frank Hurley, Maslyn Williams, and George Silk, Middle East, c. 1941
Frank Hurley 1885–1962
National Library of Australia, Canberra
© National Library of Australia

Page 60 *Australia, A Camera Study by Frank Hurley*
Angus and Robertson, Sydney, first edition, 1955

Page 233 Prestwich cinematographic 35 mm motion picture camera
Courtesy of the Scott Polar Research Institute

Page 235 Prestwich No. 5 cinematographic 35 mm hand-cranked camera
Stephen Herbert Collection

Page 236 *"Lenses. Series 3a For High Speed Subjects Cinematography. Portraits."*
Courtesy of Cooke Optical Company Archives, New Jersey, USA

Page 238 Kodak FPK No. 3a camera
Courtesy of Michael Gray
See also page 6

Page 239 *"Sydney Harbour Bridge,"* c. 1940s
Frank Hurley 1885–1962
Frank Hurley Collection
National Library of Australia, Canberra
© National Library of Australia
See also page 231